MAGNA CARTA AND OTHER ADDRESSES

MAGNA CARTA
AND OTHER ADDRESSES

BY

WILLIAM DAMERON GUTHRIE

Essay Index Reprint Series

BOOKS FOR LIBRARIES PRESS
FREEPORT, NEW YORK

First Published 1916
Reprinted 1969

STANDARD BOOK NUMBER:
8369-1082-6

LIBRARY OF CONGRESS CATALOG CARD NUMBER:
74-84309

PRINTED IN THE UNITED STATES OF AMERICA

CONTENTS

vi CONTENTS

MAGNA CARTA[1]

TO the student of American institutions it must appear singularly impressive and instructive that the members of the Constitutional Convention of the state of New York have paused in their important work to celebrate the seven-hundredth anniversary of the Great Charter of English Liberties and to look back reverently through the centuries to the sources of our constitutional law and to the days when our ancestors were laying the foundations of civil liberty and political justice. It is, indeed, no exaggeration to assert that Magna Carta marked the greatest political epoch in the history of our race, in that it saved England from becoming one of the arbitrary and degrading despotisms which arose in Europe after the overthrow of the feudal system, and that from its principles sprang representative and constitutional government, with all that these terms have grown to mean to Americans. This ceremony must again emphasize the great truth that everything which has power to win the obedience and respect of men must have its roots deep in the past, and that the more slowly institutions have grown, so much the more enduring are they likely to prove.

[1] Address before the Constitutional Convention of the state of New York at its celebration of the seven-hundredth anniversary of Magna Carta, Albany, June 15, 1915.

Two hundred and eighteen years ago the royal
governor of New York is reported to have ex-
claimed to the legislature of the colony: "There
are none of you but are big with the privileges of
Magna Carta." And to-day, Mr. President, can it
not be said with equal force and pride that there
are no Americans but are big with the privileges of
Magna Carta? Long may that continue to be true!
To provide that the spirit of these privileges shall
endure forever, so far as lies in human power, is
the highest and noblest duty of every American
constitutional convention.

Other speakers will treat of the historical and
political aspects of Magna Carta and of its reissues
and confirmations by king after king and parliament after parliament. I am to speak of the legal
value of some of the cardinal features of the Great
Charter as antecedents of principles which are
closely connected with our present political life and
which continue to invigorate our system of constitutional law. But my treatment of this large and
important aspect of the subject must necessarily
be inadequate, in view of the limited time at your
disposal.

It is undoubtedly true that Magna Carta contained much that was old in 1215 and much that
subsequently became antiquated because inapplica-
ble to changed conditions; yet it then crystallized
and served to perpetuate the fundamental principles
of the liberties of Englishmen. Solemnly confirmed
no less than thirty-seven times by seven kings of

England, it naturally became in the eyes of Englishmen the embodiment of their deepest and most firmly rooted rights and liberties and their great and stirring battle-cry against tyranny. The reissue of 1225 still remains on the English statute books as in full force and effect, so that, as an English historian has recently said, every act appearing on the statute rolls is in a sense an act amending Magna Carta.

The spirit of Magna Carta, as it thus survived, has for centuries inspired Englishmen and Americans, even though its letter may be dead and most of its provisions may long ago have become obsolete and their exact meaning hidden beneath the ruins of the past. Indeed, provisions of the Great Charter were frequently violated by king and parliament after 1215, and were allowed to fall into neglect for generations at a time; but it cannot be doubted that, if the principles they embodied had been observed, they would have secured permanent political liberty and constitutional government to England long before the seventeenth century, and that only disregard of those principles made possible the five centuries of tyranny and oppression recorded by English history.

It may likewise be true, as some historians of the scientific school are now contending, that the framers of the Great Charter and the representatives of the English church, baronage and people gathered on the meadows at Runnymede on the 15th day of June, 1215, had little or no grasp of the science of politics or of constitutional principles as we understand them. It is probably true that they had no very definite conception of the theory of representative government, or of the separation of governmental powers, or of those inalienable rights of the individual which our Declaration of Independence was later to proclaim, just as it is probably true that very few of them could even read the language in which the charter was written. But statesmen and lawyers, in dealing with the practical problems of constitutional government, will not minimize the value of Magna Carta, and our debt to the generation that forced it from King John, merely because the underlying principles may not have been fully grasped by its framers and its traditions may be based on legends and myths. It is enough that the charter contained the germ and the spirit of civil liberty and political justice.

It may be conceded that the framers of Magna Carta builded better than they knew, and likewise that many of the traditions as to the intent, meaning and scope of its provisions — traditions which were so potent and inspiring during the seventeenth and eighteenth centuries—were founded, as is now asserted, upon legends and myths. Yet, these legends and traditions, growing up and clustering around Magna Carta, served to keep alive and perpetuate its spirit. They generated the sentiment which impelled men to patriotic and heroic sacrifice in the cause of liberty; they sustained generation after generation in the recurring struggles for political justice and equality before the law; they formed and preserved a public morality which prevented violations of the principles of the Great Charter, and they were of incalculable inspiration and encouragement to Englishmen and Americans, if not to the whole world. The great traditions of Magna Carta have made its heritage peculiarly valuable and its service to humanity immortal. It is because of these traditions that Magna Carta is doubly sacred to us, as it was to our forefathers.

Many of us, however, venture to believe that the unknown author of the original Articles of the Barons or of the Great Charter itself — if it was not the learned Stephen Langton, who had been educated at the University of Paris and was familiar with Roman and canonical law and the charters of liberties which the kings of France had been granting to their subjects — knew far more of the underlying and vivifying principles of jurisprudence and politics than some of our modern critics are willing to attribute to that generation. Be this as it may, the political instinct of our race must have guided the framers to the eternal truths upon which the Great Charter of Liberties was based, even though they imperfectly comprehended these truths, or did not comprehend them at all. A single phrase like "the law of the land" in a political document is often wiser than is realized, not merely by the masses who acclaim it, but even by the leaders who write it. It may happily serve to preserve and compress into very small compass the relics of ancient wisdom, not-

withstanding the fact that later generations are frequently puzzled to decipher the contents and discover
the meaning. Such a phrase, as has been well said
of the language of a nation, "sometimes locks up
truths which were once well known, but which in
the course of ages have passed out of sight and been
forgotten. In other cases it holds the germs of truths,
of which, though they were never plainly discerned,
the genius of its framers caught a glimpse in a happy
moment of divination, . . . and often it would seem
as though rays of truths, which were still below the
intellectual horizon, had dawned upon the imagination
as it was looking up to heaven." [1]

First and foremost among the cardinal principles
of Magna Carta was the idea, then beginning again
to germinate throughout Europe, that the individual
has natural rights as against the government, and
that those rights ought to be secured to him by
fundamental laws which should be unalterable by
king or council. No one can study the history of
European politics during the great constructive thirteenth century without being impressed by the fact
of the revival of this conception in men's minds,
not only in England, but on the Continent, where it
manifested itself in varying forms and in different
connections. I say revival, because the same conviction had prevailed hundreds of years before in
both Greece and Rome; but it had been lost for
centuries.

The idea that the fundamental laws of the land

---

[1] Guesses at Truth, 1st series, 3d ed. (1847), pp. 324–325.

— the pious and good old laws of Alfred and of Edward, as the English called them, or *les lois fondamentales*, as the French were then calling them — were unalterable and that any governmental regulation, or edict, or statute to the contrary should be treated as void and null, is plainly enunciated in the first chapter of Magna Carta, where King John grants to the freemen of the kingdom "all the underwritten liberties, to be had and held by them and their heirs, of us and our heirs forever," and in chapter sixty-one, where the king covenants that he "shall procure nothing from any one, directly or indirectly, whereby any part of these concessions and liberties might be revoked or diminished; and if any such thing has been procured, let it be void and null." It is certain that during the thirteenth and fourteenth centuries the theory generally prevailed in England that the concessions and liberties of the Great Charter had been granted forever and were unalterable by the king, or even by parliament. Thus, we find parliament enacting in 1369, with the consent of Edward III., that the Great Charter of Liberties should be "holden and kept in all points, and if any statute be made to the contrary, that shall be holden for none."

One of the scholarly critics of Magna Carta suggests that this enactment of 1369 was quite an "illogical theory" on the part of parliament, because, to quote his language, "if parliament had power to alter the sacred terms of Magna Carta, it had power to alter the less sacred statute of 1369 which

declared it unalterable."[1]   The conclusive answer
to this kind of reasoning, at least as it must seem
to statesmen and lawyers, is that Magna Carta was
then regarded as something very different from and
much higher than any ordinary statute.   The people
of that day would have protested, if the logic of
parliament had then been challenged by the learned,
that Magna Carta was a permanent charter of
liberties and as such not subject to amendment or
nullification by mere statute.   But logical or illogical as the act of 42 Edward III. may have been at
the time, or may seem to be to the logicians of the
twentieth century, it serves to show that in the
fourteenth century the English people understood
and intended, and the king and parliament expressly
agreed and conceded, that the liberties guaranteed
by the Great Charter, then being again and again
confirmed, were unalterable, and that any statute
to the contrary should be "holden for none."

The spirit of that declaration still lives in every
American constitution.   We certainly have here the
antecedent of the great controlling principle underlying the whole structure of American constitutional
law, that any statute in conflict with the fundamental
laws, so far as we see fit to perpetuate them in constitutional provisions, shall be void and null, in the
language of the Great Charter, or holden for none,
in the language of the time of Edward III.   Chief
Justice Marshall in the great case of Marbury vs.
Madison, in 1803, was but following these ancient

[1] W. S. McKechnie, *Magna Carta*, 2d ed. (1914), p. 159.

declarations when, speaking for the Supreme Court
of the United States, he settled — we hope for all
time — the beneficent and indispensable doctrine
that a statute contrary to an American constitution
must be treated by the courts as void and null and
holden for none.

I do not overlook the fact that this idea of fundamental laws unchangeable by statute long slumbered
in England, and that the contrary — the legal supremacy of parliament — was subsequently established.
In studying this aspect of the Great Charter, we
must recall that the conditions of life in England
during the thirteenth and fourteenth centuries were
very much simpler than those existing later, and
that it was not then realized, or at most only vaguely
and dimly, that the legislative power could change
the laws regulating the rights and duties of individuals as among themselves or in their relation to
the government. The modern habit of imagining
that in legislation is to be found the panacea for all
ills and of measuring the efficiency of a government
by the number of statutes it has produced was
unthought of. Probably the only legislative function in the minds of Englishmen during the thirteenth
and fourteenth centuries was taxation, and as yet
men hardly realized the necessity for broader regu-
lative or legislative powers.

Nevertheless, the doctrine that the permanent
fundamental principles of the law of the land guaranteed by Magna Carta were inviolable prevailed
in England long after the fourteenth century, and

in fact was declared in the English courts as late as the seventeenth century. Bonham's case is the most familiar instance of the recognition of that doctrine. The views of English lawyers, judges and statesmen have changed in this respect, and it is now settled that parliament is supreme and that it can amend or repeal Magna Carta in any respect it may see fit. The changed view undoubtedly met with ready acquiescence, partly because of the necessity for amendments of the law in order to cope with changing conditions, partly because of the unwillingness of the English people to leave questions of constitutional power to the courts, in view of the dependence of the judges upon the crown, but principally because of the confident belief that parliament existed primarily for the very purpose of upholding and protecting the rights and liberties secured to the people by the Great Charter of Liberties, and that the people could rely upon parliament never to consent to the violation of those rights and liberties.

Repeatedly from the seventeenth century to our own day legislation has been criticized in Great Britain and Ireland on the ground that it was in conflict with Magna Carta, and always the strongest and most effective argument against proposed legislation has been that it would violate the principles of the Great Charter of Liberties. During the past thirty years thoughtful observers of English politics have remarked that private property in England is, on the whole, less secure from attack on the part of the government in our day than it was at the time of the Stuarts. Whenever the increase of class legislation and attacks on private property shall lead Englishmen to place checks and restraints upon the power of temporary majorities, so as more effectively to protect personal and property rights — an event which, I believe, must inevitably come to pass sooner or later — then the stirring battle-cry will again be Magna Carta, and the result may be a return to the spirit of the declarations of Magna Carta and of the statute of Edward III., that any statute contrary to the law of the land guaranteeing the fundamental rights and liberties of the individual shall be void and null and holden for none. And to make that ancient, sound and honest principle really an effective protection to the individual and to minorities, the courts of justice of England may at last be empowered, as they are with us, to refuse to give force and effect and to hold for none any statute in conflict with the fundamental law of the land.

Of an importance no less vital than the idea of a permanent law of the land safeguarding the fundamental rights and liberties of the individual, was the express declaration in the first chapter of Magna Carta that the English church, *Anglicana ecclesia*, should be free from interference on the part of the crown and that her rights should be entire and her liberties inviolable. In this provision we have the germ of an independent church and the idea of the separation of Church and State.

It is reasonable to assume and, in view of the surrounding circumstances and the language then employed, it is highly probable that, under the lead of Langton, who was born of English parents and intensely patriotic, probably himself the author of the clause, the churchmen of that day conceived that the religion of the English people ought to be free from governmental control, and that the English church had interests and privileges independent of the crown and independent likewise of the interests and policies of Rome. At that very time the English churchmen, in cooperating with the barons and people of England to secure Magna Carta, were acting against the will of Rome; indeed, as we know, the Pope promptly denounced the Great Charter and the patriot primate, because the Pope considered that the Great Charter was derogatory to the dignity of King John as a vassal of the Holy See. In this provision of Magna Carta relating to the English church, even though it was disregarded for centuries, we recognize the idea of religious liberty and the American political principle of the separation of Church and State, as also, though vaguely, the great principle underlying the noble declaration in our own state constitution that "the free exercise and enjoyment of religious profession and worship, without discrimination or preference, shall forever be allowed in this state to all mankind."

The provisions of the Great Charter relating to the administration of justice were undoubtedly

those which were of chief concern to the people at
large, as they were certainly, if observed, those
most essential for the security of their liberties.
The framers knew that it was in the courts that the
king of England would keep his promises, if at all,
and that the king's government would only be as
good as his judges were learned, independent and
impartial. In these provisions of Magna Carta we
find the principle of the separation and independence
of the judicial power and the soundest and highest
conceptions of the administration of justice, conceptions far in advance of those to be found in any
other document or enactment of that age.

The framers had grasped the great truth that
jurisprudence is a science, that the law must be
administered by men learned in that science and
bound to obey its rules and follow its precedents,
that uniformity and certainty are essential to the
administration of justice, and that the highest
political liberty is the right to justice according
to law and not according to the will of the judge or
the judge's master, or according to the judge's
individual discretion, or his notions of right and
wrong. They had also arrived at the conclusion
that every Englishman was entitled as of absolute
right to a day in a court which would hear before it
condemned, which would proceed upon notice and
inquiry, and which would render judgment only
after a fair trial. The plain people of England
knew full well that the struggle for their old laws —
the laws of their land, pious, good, fixed and perma-

nent, as they devoutly believed them to be — would be fruitless unless they secured permanent courts and learned, independent and impartial judges; and they instinctively felt, if they did not clearly perceive, that the law is infinitely wiser than those who may be called upon to administer it, and that, as Aristotle had declared fifteen hundred years before, "to seek to be wiser than the laws is the very thing which is by good laws forbidden."

It was Magna Carta that established in England the doctrine of the rule of law administered in fixed courts by learned and independent judges bound to obey the law; and it was Magna Carta that established the greatest of all the English constitutional doctrines, that of the supremacy of the law over every official however high. When the Great Charter was being translated and explained in the cathedrals, churches and monasteries of England, the people fully understood the tremendous significance and value to them, determined as they were to establish a rule of law and put an end to arbitrary decrees, of the famous covenant in chapter forty-five that the king would "appoint as justices, constables, sheriffs, or bailiffs only such as know the law of the realm and mean to observe it well," and of the covenants in chapter seventeen that the "common pleas shall not follow our court, but shall be held in some fixed place" — in chapter eighteen that the petty assizes should be held in the county court — in chapter thirty-six that the writ of inquisition should be freely "granted, and never denied" — in

chapter forty that "to no one will we sell, to no one
will we refuse or delay, right or justice," which in
time came to be interpreted as a universal guaranty
of free and impartial justice to all classes high and
low.

For many generations in England and in America
it was believed that the writ of habeas corpus, justly
esteemed the great bulwark of personal liberty, had
its direct guaranty or at least its antecedent in Magna
Carta. Such was the contention of counsel in the
Five Knights case of 1627, and such was the declaration of the Petition of Right of 1628. This view is
now being challenged on the ground that the exact
procedure subsequently developed was not provided
for in Magna Carta and was not in the minds of its
authors. Even if this be so, the underlying principle of chapter thirty-six and its promise that the
writ of inquisition should be freely "granted, and
never denied" naturally led in time, after the passing of trial by combat, to the right of speedy inquisition by grand jury and trial by petit jury. At all
events, the principle of the writ of habeas corpus
was for centuries assumed to be embodied in Magna
Carta.

Professor Dicey lecturing at Oxford on "The Law
of the Constitution" has well remarked that, although the English Habeas Corpus acts declare no
principle and define no rights, they are for practical
purposes worth a hundred constitutional articles
guaranteeing individual liberty. As in England,
so with us. Without the writ of habeas corpus

there would be no liberty worthy of the name and
no rights of personal freedom of any practical value.
We have only to read the leading cases in our courts
to realize how great a part the writ has played and
still plays in securing and rendering effective the
fundamental principles of American liberty.

Chapters twelve and fourteen of Magna Carta
dealt with the subject of taxation, and they laid the
foundation of our representative system and of the
separation of the legislative from the executive
power. As has been suggested, the only legislative
function that the people of England in the thirteenth
century contemplated as closely affecting them or
as likely to create any pressing grievance was that
of taxation. It was, therefore, expressly provided
in the Great Charter that, aside from the three
existing feudal aids, more or less fixed, the power to
impose taxes should not be exercised without the
consent of the *commune consilium*. This common
council is the body that fifty years later developed
into the famous parliament of Simon de Montfort
of 1265.

In the controversies in regard to taxation subsequently arising, whether in parliament, in the courts,
or in the forum of public opinion, it was always insisted that Magna Carta prevented taxation without
the consent of parliament, just as in the eighteenth
century our ancestors contended that Magna Carta
prevented taxation without representation, that is,
prevented the imposition of taxes except by a legislative body in which the taxpayers were represented.

We have only to refer to the arguments in the great constitutional cases before the courts of England in the seventeenth century, such as the famous case of Impositions in the reign of James I. and the still more famous case of Ship-Money in the reign of Charles I., to realize how much the people relied upon Magna Carta as establishing the doctrine that parliament alone could impose taxes.

The counsel for Bate in the former case and for Hampden in the latter case may not have apprehended the philosophical theory of the separation of governmental powers elaborated by Montesquieu in the next century, and they may not have contended that taxation was essentially a legislative function and, therefore, could not be exercised by the king; but in final analysis they affirmed these principles when they asserted that parliament alone could impose taxes. The judgment of a majority of the court in the Ship-Money case, as had been the judgment in the case of Impositions, was in favor of the crown, but the appeal to the country cost Charles I. his head and ultimately resulted in vesting in parliament the exclusive power to legislate and hence to tax. If England had then had an independent judiciary charged with the duty of enforcing the fundamental law of the land, the levying of the taxes in both of these cases would have been held contrary to the letter, as it was certainly contrary to the spirit, of Magna Carta.

It is no answer to say that the parliament of to-day finds its prototype not in the old common council referred to in Magna Carta, but in the parliament of 1265, nor is it an answer to say that the idea of taxation in its abstract form is essentially modern and was quite unknown in 1215. I do not suggest that the people of England in 1215 or even in 1265 understood the virtues of the representative system, or the principles of taxation or of the separation of powers. The point is that the direct consequence of the provisions of Magna Carta was a parliament based, theoretically at least, on the representative idea as well as on the principle that there could be no legislation without the consent of parliament.

The most famous of all the chapters of Magna Carta and the most important and far-reaching from a juridical point of view is undoubtedly the thirty-ninth, which provides that "no freeman shall be taken or imprisoned or disseised or exiled or in any way destroyed, nor will we go upon him nor send upon him, except by the lawful judgment of his peers or by the law of the land."

The substance of this provision as to "the law of the land," or its equivalent "due process of law," is of universal application throughout the United States as a constitutional limitation upon the powers of government, and it is to be found not only in the Constitution of the United States but in the constitution of every state of the Union. It is now firmly established in American and English constitutional law, and it is familiar knowledge, that the terms "the law of the land" and "due process of law" are exactly

MAGNA CARTA 19

equivalent in meaning and in legal force and effect. The earliest use of the phrase "due process of law" in American constitutions seems to have been in the fifth amendment to the Constitution of the United States, ratified in 1791. None of the state constitutions then in existence contained that term, but nearly all of them used the phrase "the law of the land." The phrase "due process of law" will be found in the New York bill of rights of 1787.

Until recent years, it had been assumed that the term "the lawful judgment of his peers" in Magna Carta meant trial by jury according to the modern understanding of that term, and that the term "the law of the land" meant laws conforming to those fundamental principles of justice which protect every individual in the full enjoyment of life, liberty and property secure from the arbitrary exercise of the powers of government. That is still the technical legal meaning of these two terms both in England and in America, although their practical effect and operation are different with us, because of our system of written constitutions which the legislative branch may not disregard or violate. Both of these meanings, however, are now challenged by certain critics as being without foundation in either the provisions or the history of the Great Charter.

Some historians contend that the familiar provision of Magna Carta could not have meant trial by a jury of twelve and a unanimous verdict, because such a jury, according to our present knowledge, did not exist until the second half of the fourteenth century. But it is quite immaterial whether the exact form of our jury-trial existed in England in 1215, or when the Great Charter was subsequently reissued or confirmed, provided that the foundations of the system had then been laid. It is sufficient for us that the antecedents of the modern jury system in all its three forms of grand jury, criminal jury and civil jury existed at the time of Magna Carta and were preserved by it. As the jury system developed, with the changes inevitably attending all such institutions of legal procedure and machinery, the form for the time being, whatever its exact nature, became "the lawful judgment of his peers" within the intent and meaning of the Great Charter. In any event, the latest confirmations of that instrument occurred at a time when the jury system as now in force was being firmly established. It is, therefore, easy to understand how the provision "the lawful judgment of his peers" in the course of time came to be regarded as intended to guarantee the common-law jury of twelve with unanimity in verdict.

Thus many, if not most, of our constitutional provisions now apply to conditions not at all contemplated by their framers although clearly within the principle enunciated and the spirit of the language used. Much of the efficacy of our federal and state bills of rights, or of any similar provisions which this Convention may embody in the new constitution, would be practically nullified if the language used were to be interpreted as being limited to the particular conditions existing when they were adopted. It is the spirit and the expanding principles of constitutional provisions which should always control. The letter killeth.

A charter of liberties, a bill of rights, or a constitution is not an ephemeral enactment designed to meet only the conditions existing at the time of its adoption. It embodies and perpetuates permanent principles. It is designed to endure "forever," in the language of Magna Carta, and "to approach immortality as nearly as human institutions can approach it," in the lofty phrase of Marshall, the great Chief Justice of the United States. Under any other rule of interpretation, Magna Carta would have become antiquated long before the discovery of America.

By the phrase "the law of the land," in chapter thirty-nine, the fundamental principles and axioms of the existing law were perpetuated. Exactly what those fundamental principles and axioms were then understood to be is not now capable of accurate exposition. The judges and the people of those days certainly had some definite ideas of reasonably just and fixed rules of conduct adequate for the solution of the simple questions arising in the controversies then being submitted for adjudication. Had the judges been pressed for a comprehensive or philosophical definition of "the law of the land," they might have said that they would not attempt to define the term any more than they would attempt to define justice itself, and that, as the Supreme

Court of the United States declared only a few years ago, it is better to ascertain the intent of such an important phrase in a great constitutional document by the gradual process of judicial inclusion and exclusion as practical experience may dictate and as the cases presented for decision may require; in other words, that their decisions would in time sufficiently declare and perpetuate the principles of the law of

> "A land of settled government,
> A land of just and old renown,
> Where freedom slowly broadens down
> From precedent to precedent."

The phrase "the law of the land," as used in Magna Carta, must have been intended at the time to include procedure as well as substantive law, but the term "due process of law," now its current equivalent, originally related only to procedure. A very early, if not the earliest, use of the term "due process of law" will be found in a statute of the year 1354, 28 Edward III., in which it was provided that no person should be condemned without being first brought to answer by due process of the law, the exact wording in the quaint Norman-French of the day being "*saunz estre mesne en respons par due proces de lei.*" As at the same time the Great Charter was being expressly confirmed "to be kept and maintained in all points," the provision in regard to *due proces de lei* in the act of 1354 was undoubtedly intended to be supplemental to the provisions of the Great Charter and to apply only

to persons being brought to trial in a court of justice.
It is true that in the seventeenth century Lord Coke
used the phrase "due process of law" as the equivalent of "the law of the land," but in the contemporaneous Petition of Right of 1628 mention is made
specifically of the "Great Charter of the Liberties
of England" and its provision as to "the law of the
land," and reference is made separately to the act
of 28 Edward III. and its provision that no man
should be prosecuted "without being brought to
answere by due process of lawe."

The same distinction in the use of these terms will
be found in the history of the Plymouth colony as
early as 1636 and also in the early history of the state
of New York.   The New York charter of liberties
and privileges of 1683 speaks of "being brought to
answere by due course of law," the words evidently
being taken either from the act of Edward III. of
1354, or from the Petition of Right of 1628.   The
New York constitution of 1777 used the term "the
law of the land" but did not use the term "due
process of law."   In the New York bill of rights of
1787, we find the phrases "the law of the land,"
"due process of law" and "due course of law,"
and in one section the phrase "due process of law
according to the law of the land."   Both terms,
"the law of the land" and "due process of law,"
are used with evidently the same meaning in the
present constitution of the state of New York,
that is to say, "the law of the land" is used in
section 1 of Article I. and "due process of law"

in section 6. The separate history of each section, the former first appearing in the constitution of 1777 and the latter in the constitution of 1821, will account for the difference in terminology.

It would be interesting to trace the varying uses of these terms in our forty-eight state constitutions, but that must be left for some other occasion. A majority of the state constitutions, including most of the recent constitutions, now contain the term "due process of law." As that term is the one used in the fourteenth amendment, which is applicable to all the states, it might be preferable, for the sake of uniformity and certainty, to adopt that form as less likely to confuse. Moreover, the phrase "due process of law" lends itself readily to a more comprehensive and inclusive definition if we define the word "due" to mean *just and appropriate* and the word "process" to mean *substantive provision* as well as procedure.

Finally, it may be of interest to notice the sanction and security devised for enforcing the covenants of Magna Carta. A body or tribunal of twenty-five barons, called executors, was created by chapter sixty-one, who were to "be bound with all their might, to observe and hold, and cause to be observed, the peace and liberties we have granted and confirmed to them," and who were to have power to compel the king himself, even by force, to keep the promises he had made. The clause providing this security or legal sanction was crude, but it was not necessarily an impracticable innovation. Although the plan utterly failed, it remained of immense value in principle. That principle established the right of the subjects to compel the king of England to obey a body of fixed laws outside and beyond his will; it justified revolution for just cause, and it inspired our forefathers in their struggle against George III. The influence of this idea upon public sentiment as justifying revolution, particularly during the seventeenth and eighteenth centuries, cannot well be over-estimated. The ineffectiveness of this provision of Magna Carta served also to demonstrate the futility of such a tribunal and security, and to lead the English people to look thereafter solely to the courts of justice and to parliament for the protection of their rights and liberties. The founders of our own republican governments may have been warned by the failure of this sanction that it would be unwise to create any political body with power to enforce constitutional provisions, and it may have been for this reason that they left the enforcement of constitutional limitations and the protection of the individual and minorities to an independent non-political forum composed of impartial judges learned in the law and meaning "to observe it well," according to the spirit of Magna Carta.

In closing his great commentaries on the Constitution of the United States, Mr. Justice Story admonished the American people that, although the whole structure of our constitutional liberty was erected by architects of consummate skill and fidelity, with its defences impregnable from without, it might nevertheless perish in an hour by the folly or corruption or negligence of its only keepers, the people. It cannot, indeed, be too often declared that, if constitutional government and fundamental rights are to endure, they must be maintained and preserved by competent leaders and representatives of the people constantly teaching the value of the traditions of Magna Carta and the necessity of adhering to constitutional principles and observing constitutional morality. The members of this Convention are not likely to disregard the living spirit of the Great Charter of English Liberties and its enduring value to Americans. It was Lincoln who said that "as a nation of freemen we must live through all time, or die by suicide." But we shall perpetuate free government and civil liberty only as we adhere to two essential conditions: the one, that our fundamental rights shall continue to be inviolable by the state, the other, that they shall be equal. "If not inviolable, they are not rights, but only enjoyments on sufferance; if not equal, they are but the privileges of a class, whatever that class may be."[1]

[1] Edward J. Phelps, Orations and Essays (1901), p. 127.

THE MAYFLOWER COMPACT [1]

WHEREVER Americans gather, at home or abroad, those who can claim the proud heritage of descent from the Pilgrims on the Mayflower are accustomed annually to join in thanksgiving for all that they owe to their ancestors. The spirit which prompts these celebrations is singularly wholesome, and indeed holy. Among the natural instincts of the heart, common to all races, is a longing for communion with the past, which manifests itself in the worship of ancestors. That this spirit of reverence has been from the earliest ages a most powerful religious and patriotic force is a fact familiar to us in the history of the Egyptians, the Greeks and the Romans. We readily recall the beautiful ceremonial of pagan Rome on the *dies parentales*, when violets and roses and wine, oil and milk were offered and *aves* were chanted to the spirits of their dead.

An impressive example of the survival of this instinct in modern times is afforded by the Japanese, who daily, at innumerable household shrines and public temples erected to Shintō, worship their

[1] Remarks responding to the toast, "The Mayflower Compact," at the twenty-first annual banquet of the Society of Mayflower Descendants in the State of New York, held at the Hotel St. Regis, New York, November 23, 1915.

ancestors as the gods of the home and of the nation. When, twenty-years ago, Japan so easily defeated the Chinese Empire with ten times the population of Japan, the surprise and marvel of the world impelled one of the most brilliant writers of our generation to seek the source of the fortitude, the indomitable spirit and the military valor of the Japanese. He did not expect to find it in their form of government or in their laws, for he realized the great truth that mere forms of government and laws possess no magical or supernatural virtue and are of little moment in nations in comparison with the moral character of their leaders and their people. He discovered, as he believed, that the secret of the civil and martial power of the Japanese and the source of their moral energy and virtue — I use virtue in the Latin sense of valor — lay in the vital and all-pervading worship of their ancestors, based upon the deep-rooted belief that all things are determined by the dead. He found that this homage excited at once the deepest emotion and the most powerful inspiration of the race, shaping their national character, directing their national life, teaching them reverence, obedience, self-restraint, temperance, loyalty, courage, devotion and sacrifice, and making them ever conscious of the prodigious debt the present owes to the past, as well as keenly sensible of the duty of love and gratitude to the departed for their labors and suffering. "They," the dead, he eloquently wrote, "created all that we call civilization, — trusting us to correct such mistakes as they could not help making. The sum of their toil is incalculable; and all that they have given us ought surely to be very sacred, very precious, if only by reason of the infinite pain and thought which it cost." And then he added, "Yet what Occidental dreams of saying daily, like the Shintō believer: *'Ye forefathers of the generations, and of our families, and of our kindred, — unto you, the founders of our homes, we utter the gladness of our thanks'?"* [1]

In the reverential spirit so beautifully expressed by this Japanese prayer, I venture upon a necessarily brief and imperfect review of a subject of transcendent and enduring interest to Americans — the debt that American constitutional government, under which we enjoy the blessings of civil and religious liberty and of just and equal laws, owes to your ancestors of the Mayflower.

In these days of superlative comfort and affluence, it is difficult for us assembled in this palatial hall, feasting better than the Cæsars feasted and served as not even princes were served three hundred years ago — difficult, if not impossible, is it to carry our minds from this gorgeous and almost oppressive luxury back through the centuries to November, 1620, to the Mayflower covered with snow and ice and buffeted by fierce winter winds off the bleak and desolate coast of Cape Cod. Equally difficult is it to picture to ourselves and in imagination to breathe the air of that first American constitutional convention, in the cramped and chilling cabin of

[1] Lafcadio Hearn, *Kokoro*, pp. 289–290.

the Mayflower, when the Pilgrim Fathers were assisting, as Bancroft says, at "the birth of popular constitutional liberty," and were discussing the provisions of what has since been called the first written constitution ever framed by a people for their own government from the time history began to record human politics and human successes and failures. I need not stop to read the contents of the completed draft of that constitution, conceived in the then vague prompting, which one hundred and fifty-six years later was to be proclaimed in our Declaration of Independence as a self-evident truth, that all governments must derive "their just powers from the consent of the governed." Nor shall I read the names of the forty-one immortals who executed that compact in order to evidence their covenant of due consent and promise of obedience to its provisions and spirit. Surely, if there be one constitutional document which should be familiar to all Americans, and particularly to the descendants of the Pilgrims, it is the Mayflower Compact of November 21, 1620.[1]

[1] The original manuscript of the Mayflower Compact has been lost or destroyed. The text, as preserved by Governor Bradford in his annals entitled "Of Plimoth Plantation," is as follows:

"In ye name of God, Amen. We whose names are under-writen, the loyall subjects of our dread soveraigne Lord, King James, by ye grace of God, of Great Britaine, Franc, & Ireland king, defender of ye faith, &c., haveing undertaken, for ye glorie of God, and advancemente of ye Christian faith, and honour of our king & countrie, a voyage to plant ye first colonie in ye Northerne parts of Virginia, doe by those presents solemnly & mutualy in ye presence of God, and one of another, covenant & combine our selves togeather into a civill body politick, for our better ordering & preservation & furtherance of ye ends aforesaid; and by vertue hearof to

Many of us believe that the compact thus entered into was the prototype of the Constitution of the United States, that the government it established was the beginning of the republican form of government now guaranteed alike to nation and state, and that the covenant it contained for just and equal laws was the germ from which has since developed our whole system of constitutional jurisprudence. This covenant reads: "We . . . doe by these presents solemnly & mutualy in ye presence of God, and one of another, covenant & combine our selves togeather into a civill body politick, for our better ordering & preservation & furtherance of ye ends aforesaid; and by vertue hearof to enacte, constitute, and frame such just & equall lawes, ordinances, acts, constitutions, & offices, from time to time, as shall be thought most meete & convenient for ye generall good of y^c Colonie, unto which we promise all due submission and obedience." Surely, this simple, comprehensive and lofty language, in the style of the Bible open before the Pilgrims, embodies the true and invigorating spirit of our constitutional polity as it flourishes to-day.

enacte, constitute, and frame such just & equall lawes, ordinances, acts, constitutions, & offices, from time to time, as shall be thought most meete & convenient for ye generall good of ye Colonie, unto which we promise all due submission and obedience. In witnes wherof we have hereunder subscribed our names at Cap-Codd ye 11. of November, in ye year of ye raigne of our soveraigne lord, King James, of England, France, & Ireland ye eighteenth, and of Scotland ye fiftie fourth. An^o: Dom. 1620." Printed in the Collections of the Massachusetts Historical Society, 4th series, vol. III, pp. 89–90. See also the text in Bradford's History of Plymouth Plantation, ed. W. T. Davis (1908), p. 107.

In order to appreciate the political greatness and the moral grandeur of the work of the Pilgrims, we should recall that, when the Mayflower Compact was framed, in no part of the world did there exist a government of just and equal laws, and that in no country was there real religious liberty or the complete separation of Church and State.

In fact, the great and now fundamental principle of the separation of Church and State was first made a living reality by the Pilgrims, although, in theory at least, it antedated the voyage of the Mayflower. It was the essence of their holy covenant of congregation entered into years before. And to the Pilgrims chiefly are due the credit and honor of incorporating this principle into Anglo-American polity. A wide gulf separated the Pilgrims from the Puritans in this respect. The Pilgrims, first known in England as the Separatists and Brownists—hated alike by Puritan and Cavalier — advocated religious liberty and the complete separation of Church and State. The Puritans, however, when they secured power in England and later in New England, were intolerant in religion and opposed both to religious liberty and to the separation of Church and State. They were determined that the state should dominate in religious as well as in civil affairs and that it should regulate the religion of all; in truth, they sought to impose a dominant theocracy as completely as Henry VIII. and Elizabeth were determined to have a state church under their own spiritual supremacy and to abolish all "diversity of opinions,"

if necessary by rack, fire and the scaffold. The
Pilgrim, personifying him as you love to in the
lofty and generous spirit of Robinson at Leyden,
believed in religious freedom, or, as it is differently
phrased, in liberty of conscience; the Puritan was
determined that all should be coerced by legislation
and the sword to conform to his religious views as
the only true faith. Although the Puritan theocracy found its most complete development and
tyranny in Massachusetts, the colony of Plymouth
remained liberal and tolerant. Notwithstanding
the terrible record of sanguinary persecutions among
other religious denominations of that age, no
instance is recorded of religious persecution by the
Pilgrims or in the Plymouth colony.[1] You will
recall that the famous Pilgrim captain, Myles
Standish, never joined the Plymouth church, that
no witches were ever burned in Plymouth, and that
when a malicious woman accused a neighbor of
witchcraft, she was promptly convicted of slander
and thereupon fined and publicly whipped. The ex-
cesses and fury of religious persecution by Protestants
and Catholics alike were the products of the fierce,
intolerant and blind spirit of that age. We should
judge them not by the standards of the twentieth
century, but by those of the sixteenth and seventeenth centuries, and must not overlook the fact

[1] The legislation against the Quakers as enforced in the Plymouth
colony seems to have been essentially political. The records, so far as we
have them, indicate that the Quakers were proceeded against because of
their attempts to disturb the peace and overthrow established law and
order, and not because of their religious beliefs.

that in many cases these persecutions were as much political as they were religious.

In the history of New England the Pilgrim is often confused with the Puritan, undoubtedly because the Puritan soon dominated and ultimately absorbed the Pilgrim. Nevertheless, the differences between them on this question of religious tolerance and the separation of Church and State were implacable, to adopt the word of a great American historian. Yet, in differentiating between Pilgrim and Puritan and in recalling the facts as to the origin of religious freedom and the separation of Church and State, the greatest of all the blessings we now enjoy — in giving most of the glory to the Pilgrims, notwithstanding the claims of Catholic Maryland — I am not at all unmindful that in religion and in politics the Pilgrim and the Puritan had many views in common, that our debt to both is quite inseparable, and that our gratitude to them should be eternal.

It is certainly impossible to exaggerate the debt we owe to the Puritan spirit — fierce, indomitable and undaunted, even if intolerant, for it was that spirit which cemented the foundations of our nation. It was the Puritan spirit that gave to England her noblest figures and her most inspiring traditions of battlefields. Towering above all other Englishmen is the lofty figure of the Puritan Cromwell, and second only to him are the Puritans Hampden, Pym, Selden, Milton, Vane, Hale. Hampden — the highest type of English gentleman, with a nobility and fearlessness of character, self-control,

soundness of judgment and perfect rectitude of
intention, to which, as Macaulay declared, "the
history of revolutions furnishes no parallel or furnishes a parallel in Washington alone." If to-day
England is to preserve her empire, upon which she
boasts the sun never sets, she must appeal to the
energy and fortitude and courage of the Puritan.
She must invoke the spirit of Oliver Cromwell,
whose mighty arm made the name of England
terrible to her enemies and laid the foundations of
her empire, who led her to conquest, who never
fought a battle without gaining it, whose soldiers'
backs no enemy ever saw, who humbled Spain on
the land and Holland on the sea, and who left a
tradition of military valor which is now the inspiration of the splendid courage, heroism and
sacrifice of England's soldiers on the continent of
Europe.

A most important aspect of the Pilgrims' contribution to our political institutions is the provision for
just and equal laws contained in the Mayflower
Compact, for, as I have already suggested, in that
provision is embodied the essence of our whole
constitutional system. It has become a truism that
the characteristic of the American system of constitutional government is equality before the law. We
Americans accept this doctrine as of course. But
we should appreciate that civil equality or equality
before the law was practically unknown in Europe
when the Mayflower Compact was written. In this
country its development sprang in great measure

gradually from the seed first sown by the Pilgrims. Neither the phrase "equality before the law," so familiar to us as expressing a fundamental and self-evident truth, nor the term "the equal protection of the laws," now contained in the fourteenth amendment, is to be found in the English common law. Nor was either term, or any equivalent, in legal use in America at the time of the adoption of the Constitution of the United States. Indeed, the phrase "equality before the law" is said to be a modern translation from the French. Nevertheless, equality in duty, in right, in burden and in protection is the thought which has run through all our constitutional enactments from the beginning.

The Pilgrim Fathers perceived, long before it was generally appreciated, that equal laws might fall far short of political justice and liberty, and hence they provided for "just and equal laws." They realized, perhaps indistinctly, that equality in itself, without other elements, is not sufficient to guarantee justice, and that, under a law which is merely *equal*, all may be equally oppressed, equally degraded, equally enslaved. They well knew that equality is one of the pervading features of most despotisms, and that a law may be equal and yet be grossly arbitrary, tyrannical and unjust. Obviously, a law confiscating all property of a certain kind would be equal if it applied to all having that particular kind of property. The laws of England then in force providing for one form of worship, "for abolishing diversity of opinions," as the title of the act of 31 Henry VIII. recited, or compelling

all to attend the same church and to take the same
oath of religious supremacy and the sacraments of
the same religious denomination, were all equal
laws, because they applied to every one, no matter
what his conscience might dictate. In the cabin of
the Mayflower, the Pilgrim Fathers seem to have
had a vision revealing to them the fundamental and
essential political truth that equality is but an attribute of the liberty they were then seeking at
the peril of their lives and the sacrifice of their
fortunes, and that true liberty requires *just* as well
as *equal* laws. To repeat, it was the Pilgrims who
first sowed in our soil the seed of just and equal
laws, and that seed has grown into the fixed rule
of the American constitutional system, a rule which
has spread through all our political and civil rights
and duties until it reaches, pervades, unites and
invigorates the whole body politic.

The history of the Plymouth colony from 1620
until its absorption by the colony of Massachusetts
in 1691, teaches us many lessons in political philosophy. There are two which I desire to recall to
you to-night: one as to the right to private property,
the other as to pure democracy.

The Pilgrims began government under the Mayflower Compact with a system of communism or
common property. The experiment almost wrecked
the colony. As early as 1623, they had to discard
it and restore the old law of individual property with
its inducement and incentive to personal effort. All
who now urge communism in one form or another,

often in disguise, might profitably study the experience
of Plymouth, which followed a similarly unfortunate
and disastrous experiment in Virginia. History often
teaches men in vain. Governor Bradford's account
of this early experiment in communism in his annals
of "Plimoth Plantation" is extremely interesting.
The book is rich in political principles as true to-
day as they were three hundred years ago. After
showing that the communal system was a complete
failure and that as soon as it was abandoned and a
parcel of land was assigned in severalty to each
family, those who had previously refused to work
became "very industrious," even the women going
"willingly into yᵉ feild" taking "their litle-ons
with them to set corne, which before would aledg
weaknes, and inabilitie," Bradford proceeds as
follows:

"The experience that was had in this comͦone
course and condition, tried sundrie years, and that
amongst godly and sober men, may well evince
the vanitie of that conceite of Platos & other
ancients, applauded by some of later times; — that
yᵉ taking away of propertie, and bringing in comͤu-
nitie into a comone wealth, would make them
happy and florishing; as if they were wiser then
God. For this comunitie (so farr as it was) was
found to breed much confusion & discontent, and
retard much imploymͤt that would have been to
their benefite and comforte. For yᵉ yong-men that
were most able and fitte for labour & service did
repine that they should spend their time & streingth

to worke for other mens wives and children, with
out any recompence. The strong, or man of parts,
had no more in devission of victails & cloaths, then
he that was weake and not able to doe a quarter y^e
other could; this was thought injuestice. The aged
and graver men to be ranked and equalised in
labours, and victails, cloaths, &c., with ye meaner
& yonger sorte, thought it some indignite & disrespect
unto them. . . . Let none objecte this is men's
corruption, and nothing to ye course it selfe. I
answer, seeing all men have this corruption in
them, God in his wisdome saw another course fiter
for them." [1]

Although the colony of Plymouth began as a pure
democracy under which all the men were convened
to decide executive and judicial questions, the increase of population and its diffusion over a wider
territory necessarily led to the transaction of official
business through chosen representatives. The representative system was thus established by the Pilgrims in New England perhaps more firmly than
elsewhere, and it became the cardinal principle of
whatever efficiency, strength and stability our republican governments now have. This system is men-
aced by the enthusiasm for change and by the fads
of recent years, such as the initiative, the referendum, the recall and direct primaries. In these political nostrums has been revived the crude notion
that the masses, inexperienced as they are in the

[1] Collections of the Massachusetts Historical Society, 4th series, vol. III,
pp. 134–136.

difficult and complex problems of government, are instinctively better qualified to guide than the educated few who are trained, instructed and competent, and who, acting as the representatives of all, are bound in good conscience and sound policy to consider and protect the rights of the minority, of the individual, of the humble and weak, against the arbitrary will or selfish interest or prejudice of the majority.

There is no time to-night, even if your patience would bear with me longer, to trace the growth of the political principles which we find in the history of the Plymouth colony and underlying the experiment in republican government there initiated under the Mayflower Compact. If the tree is to be judged by its fruit, the framing of that compact in 1620 was one of the most important events in the history of the American people, and the document itself is one of the most interesting and inspiring of American constitutional documents. But I feel that I may appropriately suggest to you questions which are of immediate and urgent concern to us all, and they are whether the quickening and stirring message of the Mayflower has really endured — whether the sterling qualities of the Pilgrim and the Puritan have survived — whether the descendants of the Pilgrims have inherited and can perpetuate the invincible spirit, the unconquerable moral energy, the indomitable steadfastness of their ancestors — and whether these qualities are available in our own day to guide the nation safely and wisely through the inevitable crisis which we are approaching as the whole civilization of Europe is being daily more and more engulfed in the abyss of this awful war. These are problems which our generation must face sooner or later. And who should be better qualified to guide us — for it is leadership that we need — than men who inherit the spirit and the traditions of the Pilgrim and the Puritan?

In this crisis, the greatest in our national affairs since 1861, I hope we shall profit by the example of the founders of Plymouth, who, as Palfrey wrote, "gave diligent heed to arrangements for the military defence of the colony." It may be also that Providence will give us, in the descendant of a Pilgrim, the captain who shall be both our shield and our weapon as Myles Standish was the shield and the weapon of your ancestors.

CONSTITUTIONAL MORALITY [1]

THE text of this address is taken from Grote's "History of Greece." The historian, reviewing the state of the Athenian democracy in the age of Kleisthenes, points out that it became necessary to create in the multitude, and through them to force upon the leading men, the rare and difficult sentiment which he terms constitutional morality. He shows that the essence of this sentiment is self-imposed restraint, that few sentiments are more difficult to establish in a community, and that its diffusion, not merely among the majority, but throughout all classes, is the indispensable condition of a government at once free, stable and peaceable. Whoever has studied the history of Greece knows that the Grecian democracy was ultimately overthrown by the acts of her own citizens and their disregard of constitutional morality rather than by the spears of her conquerors.

We American lawyers would be blind, indeed, if we did not recognize that there is at the present time a growing tendency throughout the country to disregard constitutional morality. On all sides we find impatience with constitutional restraints, manifesting itself in many forms and under many

[1] Address before the Pennsylvania State Bar Association at its eighteenth annual meeting, held at Cape May, New Jersey, June 25, 1912.

pretences, and this impatience is particularly strong
with the action of the courts in protecting the individual and the minority against unconstitutional
enactments favoring one class at the expense of
another. However worded and however concealed
under professions of social reform or social justice,
the underlying spirit in most instances is that of
impatience with any restraint or rule of law.

We are meeting again the oldest and the strongest
political plea of the demagogue, so often shown to
be the most fallacious and dangerous doctrine that
has ever appeared among men, that the people are
infallible and can do no wrong, that their cry must
be taken as the voice of God, and that whatever at
any time seems to be the will of the majority, however ignorant and prejudiced, must be accepted as
gospel. The principal political battle-cry to-day
seems to be that, if the people are now fit to
rule themselves, they no longer need any checks or
restraints, that the constitutional form of representative government under which we have lived
and prospered has become antiquated and unsatis-
factory to the masses, and that we should adopt a
pure democracy and leave to the majority itself
the decision of every question of government or legislation, with the power to enforce its will or impulse
immediately and without restraint.

We find many political and social reformers advo-
cating an absolute legislative body, whose edicts, in
response to the wishes, interests, or prejudices of the
majority, shall at once become binding on all, no

matter how unjust or oppressive these edicts may be. Those who are loudest in thus demanding the supremacy of the legislative power are equally loud in charging that our legislatures are inefficient or corrupt and in proclaiming distrust of the people's representatives in legislative bodies. In one breath we are asked to vest legislatures with power and discretion beyond the control of the courts, and in the next breath we are told that legislative bodies are not to be trusted by the people, and hence that we must have the initiative and the referendum.

Other reformers would vest greater power in the executive, so as to enable him to dictate to legislatures whatever he deemed or professed to think best for the common welfare or for social progress. In the final analysis this would, of course, reduce us to a despotism pure and simple, and place Congress and the state legislatures in the condition of the Roman senate in the second century. Argue as we may from the admonitions and experience of the past, the defiant answer is that the people will select the executive and are prepared to trust him, an answer that singularly disregards the fact that they now select the legislators whom they no longer trust, and that practical reform in legislation is ready to their hand if they will only insist upon character and ability in their representatives.

Others again would deny to the courts the power and duty to declare unconstitutional and void any enactment of a legislative body that was in conflict with the constitution, or, if not going quite so far, would give the courts power to disregard constitutional limitations whenever the judges found or fancied that an enactment was in consonance with prevailing morality or the opinion of the majority in respect of matters relating to the police power or social progress or social justice. They would have the judiciary interpret and enforce a constitution not according to the mandate of the people who adopted it, nor according to the true meaning and intent of the language employed by the framers, nor according to settled general rules and principles, but according to the ever-changing desires or notions or opinions of the majority and the personal ideas of so-called progressive or sympathetic judges. Many of those who charge the judiciary with having usurped the power to determine whether a particular enactment does or does not conflict with the fundamental and supreme law as established by the people themselves, would now place a far greater power in the hands of the courts by authorizing them to expand or contract a constitution by judicial construction, and would thus in reality vest in the judges an arbitrary discretion. Under this doctrine, practically every constitutional restraint could be readily circumvented, perverted, or nullified; constitutional rights could be frittered away, and great landmarks of human progress could be undermined.

We should then have government by the judiciary with a vengeance. Our constitutional system would be no longer reasonably fixed and stable, no longer regulated by the justice of necessary general rules, but would be subject to constant uncertainty and change as judges might think the moral atmosphere of the moment or the will or opinion or interests of the majority required. It would, of course, be better to have no constitutional restraints at all, and to vest supreme power and corresponding responsibility in the legislative branch of our government. It is of the essence of judicial power that judges in deciding cases shall be bound by principles, rules and precedents, that they shall not be permitted to exercise arbitrary discretion, and that they shall be required to give reasons for their decisions. A court bound by no rules or principles at all would not be exercising judicial power as we understand that term. If we were to vest in legislatures or courts the discretion to obey or disobey constitutional restraints according as the prevailing moral or political sentiment might seem to dictate, we would at once deprive such restraints of all practical force and effect, and would have a constitution only in name and form and not in substance. As the late Chief Justice Fuller, *clarum et venerabile nomen*, so well said in the Lottery case, "our form of government may remain notwithstanding legislation or decision, but, as long ago observed, it is with governments as with religions, the form may survive the substance of the faith."[1]

The limited time at my disposal compels me to confine this address to the aspect of constitutional morality which is presented by the criticism of the

[1] 188 United States Reports, p. 375.

courts for refusing to enforce unconstitutional statutes. This seems to me to be the most dangerous of all the lines of attack. I regret that I have not time to deal with other important aspects of my subject, such as the movement for the recall of judges and judicial decisions, the agitation for the initiative and the referendum, and the growing practice on the part of legislatures and executives of abandoning the consideration of constitutional questions and leaving this duty to the courts, thus casting upon the judges the sole responsibility and frequently the unpopularity and even odium of enforcing constitutional restraints.

Few of us, I assume, would seriously suggest that the judicial department is to be above criticism, or that it is to be deemed sacrosanct so that we must bow and submit in silence, without the right of challenge, criticism, or censure, to whatever the courts declare to be law. Such a view would be absurd. Of course, judges make mistakes as the wisest and best men make mistakes. They are not infallible. But neither are our legislative bodies infallible, nor is the crowd. There must be the fullest liberty of criticism and if need be of censure of our judges as of all other public officials. Fair and just criticism, however, would be distinctly educational, and it could tend only to restore the courts to public favor and confidence. The danger is not in freedom of criticism, but in unfair and unfounded criticism supported by distorted or false statements. Our judicial system is inherently sound enough and strong enough to withstand and overcome any fair criticism. We should, therefore, encourage the fullest discussion of judicial decisions in constitutional cases in order that constitutional principles may be adequately explained and the necessity for the observance of constitutional morality brought home to the people. Let us, however, insist that the facts be truthfully stated. If the reasons and principles of justice which support most of the decisions criticized could be explained to all classes in simple language and in terms intelligible to laymen as well as to lawyers, much of the misapprehension of judicial decisions and prejudice against the courts and constitutional restraints would be dispelled. To tell the man in the street or in the workshop that a statute is in conflict with the guaranty of due process of law or of the law of the land, conveys no meaning to his mind; yet, if he understood the fundamental principles involved and the consequences of disregarding them, he might be persuaded of the justice and propriety of the decision under discussion.

I shall call your attention to a few examples of alleged abuse or usurpation of power by the judiciary, and endeavor to show the characteristics of much of the criticism of the judges and the manner in which the masses are being constantly prejudiced and inflamed against the courts.

The case in the New York courts which probably is being more criticized and misrepresented than any other is known as the Tenement House Tobacco case (Matter of Jacobs),[1] decided in January, 1885. The courts then held unconstitutional an act which forbade the manufacture of tobacco products in certain tenement houses in New York and Brooklyn, because the statute unwarrantably and unreasonably interfered with the liberty of the individual. The enactment was an attempt on the part of the owners of large tobacco factories to destroy the competition of cigar manufacturers who worked at home. It was not an honest health measure at all; it was not in fact designed to protect the health of tobacco workers, and it did not contain a single provision tending in any degree to secure sanitary conditions of work or living. Not one word in the opinions of the courts in the Jacobs case prevented the legislature from adopting regulations to secure wholesome conditions in the manufacture of any article. Since that decision, the New York constitution has been carefully revised by a constitutional convention in 1894, and in addition has been repeatedly amended, no less than nineteen separate amendments having been adopted by the people, whilst a large number of additional proposed amendments have been rejected. But in neither the revision nor in any of the amendments, whether adopted or rejected, was any change suggested in the rule of constitutional law declared in the Tenement House case, although the subject was directly called to the attention of the convention. For more than a quarter of a century, the people of the state of

[1] 98 New York Reports, p. 98.

New York have acquiesced in the decision of the
Court of Appeals as fair, just and satisfactory.

Jacobs with his wife and two children lived in a
tenement house in the city of New York and occu-
pied an apartment of seven rooms in a building
where there were only three other apartments, all
of equal size. In this apartment he carried on the
trade of manufacturing cigars, and the rooms in
which he did so were separated from the sleeping and
cooking-rooms. The testimony showed that there
was no odor of tobacco in these sleeping and cooking-
rooms. The conditions under which he was carrying
on his trade in his own home for the support of himself and his family were much more healthful than if
he and his assistants had been compelled to work in
a crowded factory, particularly in 1884, when there
were no such sanitary conditions in factories as now
prevail under the beneficent operation of our present
public health and labor laws. It was shown that,
when this legislation was enacted, 840,000,000 cigars
were being manufactured annually in the city of New
York, of which about 370,000,000, or 44 per cent.,
were made in the homes of dwellers in tenement or
apartment houses, and that about two thousand
artisans were supporting themselves and their families
by thus working at home. The board of health
of the city of New York had officially declared,
after careful investigation, as set forth in the brief
of Mr. Evarts, then the leader of the American bar,
" that the health of the tenement-house population
is not jeopardized by the manufacture of cigars in

those houses; that this bill is not a sanitary measure, and that it has not been approved by this board." It also appeared from this brief that while the death-rate in the city of New York generally was 31 in each 1,000, it was only 9 in each 1,000 in the tenement houses where cigars were being manufactured. The act, if valid and enforceable, would have crushed the competition of home workers with the tobacco factories; it would have deprived the tenement-house dweller of the liberty to exercise his trade of cigar-making at home even under the most sanitary conditions, and it would have driven every such workman and the working members of his family into crowded and generally unhealthful factories, to be harassed and oppressed by strikes and lockouts and the other troubles which attend modern labor conditions, to say nothing of being exposed to all the mischiefs, physical and moral, that are inseparable from crowded workshops. The court held that the statute was not a legitimate health regulation and released Jacobs from imprisonment. The principle of constitutional law recognized and applied was that an individual cannot be made a criminal for working at a lawful trade in his own home under sanitary conditions, and cannot be compelled by discriminatory legislation to labor in a crowded factory. If the provisions of the act had not been declared to be in conflict with the constitutional guaranty of personal liberty, similar statutes could have been passed with respect to all kinds of home work, and all artisans, whether men or women, could have

been driven into factories at the dictation of factory
owners or trade-unions having sufficient political
influence to secure the necessary legislation.

I digress here a moment to point out that people
urging particular enactments too often overlook
the effect of disregarding a principle and establishing a precedent. Constitutions declare general
rules or principles of justice, which sometimes do
not coincide with the justice of particular cases.
The framing of general rules of conduct so as to
bring about practical justice in the greatest number
of cases and with the fewest exceptions, constitutes
the science of jurisprudence, of which constitution-
making is but a branch, and the application of
these general rules to practical affairs is the duty
of legislatures and courts. The statutes before
the courts are frequently recognized and conceded
to be only entering wedges and experiments, and,
if sustained, are certain to be followed by others
far broader and more radical. If legislative power
exists to regulate a subject, the extent or degree of
its exercise is essentially for the legislature to determine in its discretion and cannot be controlled
by the courts. Hence, a court must always consider,
in determining the constitutionality of a statute,
not merely the features of the particular statute
before it and not merely the justice or merits of the
particular case as between man and man or between
the state and the individual, but what might be
done under the same principle if the statute before
it were upheld and a precedent established. Thus,

if we once grant the power of a legislature to prohibit work at home under sanitary conditions in one trade, then every trade becomes subject to the same power of regulation and prohibition, and all working men and women can be driven into crowded factories.

In the Jacobs case, Presiding Justice Noah Davis, speaking for the intermediate appellate court sitting in the city of New York, and undoubtedly acquainted with conditions then and there existing, used the following language: "A careful study of the act has satisfied us that its aim was not 'to improve the public health by prohibiting the manufacture of cigars and preparation of tobacco in any form in tenement houses in certain cases, and regulating the use of tenement houses in certain cases,' as declared in the title, but to suppress and restrain such manufacture in the cases covered by the act for the purpose of preventing successful competition injurious to other modes of manufacturing the same articles. . . . If the act were general and aimed at all tenement houses, and prohibited for sanitary reasons the manufacture of cigars and tobacco in all such buildings, or if it prohibited such manufacture in the living-rooms of all tenants, another case would be presented. But in the form in which it comes before us it is so unjust in its inequality, so harsh and oppressive upon the labor of poverty, so keenly discriminative in favor of the stronger classes engaged in the same occupation, that it certainly ought not to have been enacted; but,

being enacted, ought to be held invalid because it
deprives the appellant of his right and liberty to
use his occupation in his own house for the support
of himself and family, and takes away the value of
his labor, which is his property protected by the
Constitution equally as though it were in lands or
money, without due process of law." [1]

Discussing the Jacobs case, Mr. P. Tecumseh
Sherman of the New York bar, who is reputed to be
one of the best informed men in our state upon the
subject of labor conditions and labor legislation and
who was at one time a state commissioner of labor,
said in a letter published a few weeks ago that the
tenement-house statute, although purporting to be
for the public health, was not a reasonable regulation
for that purpose, because it arbitrarily selected one
article and forbade its manufacture under certain
conditions not generally unsanitary, and he added
that "as matter of fact, the act was not designed
to protect health but to put out of business one set
of competitors in a trade war."

Now let me call your attention to two examples of
the manner in which this decision is being criticized.
In an address delivered at Yale University last
month, the mayor of the city of New York, who for
many years had been a justice of the state supreme
court, criticized the courts and derided the administration of justice in his own state. He referred to
the Jacobs case in the following language: "The first
case I shall call your attention to is known in my

[1] 33 Hun's Reports, pp. 380, 382, 383.

own state as the Tenement House Tobacco case. . . .
You know what a condensed population we have
in a part of the city of New York. Well, benevolent men and women in going around there found
in little rooms in these crowded tenements certain
things being manufactured that were not wholesome. They found tobacco being manufactured
into its various products in the living-rooms of
these poor tenements. Benevolent people who
helped the poor saw it and they saw the evils of it.
They saw little children born into this world and
brought up in bedrooms and kitchens in the fumes
and odors of tobacco. They also saw longer hours
of work than would be the case if workers left their
work at the shop and went home. So they went
to the legislature and got a law passed forbidding
the manufacture of tobacco in the living-rooms of
these tenements." Mayor Gaynor then proceeded
to criticize and condemn the Court of Appeals for
its reasoning and decision.

The facts, however, were that the statute was
not limited to "the living-rooms of these tenements,"
but applied to every room, and that the promoters
of this legislation were not the benevolent men
and women who visit and help the poor, as Mayor
Gaynor imagined, but the owners of tobacco factories who desired to crush the competition of
independent workers. Nor was there anything in
the case before the courts to support the statement
that any one had seen "little children born into
this world and brought up in bedrooms and kitchens

in the fumes and odors of tobacco." No such conditions were before the courts, and the contrary was proved by unimpeached evidence in the Jacobs case, as any one reading the record could see. But, even if the picture had been true, the decision in this case did not in any way whatever prevent proper legislation prohibiting the manufacture of tobacco products in the bedrooms and kitchens of crowded tenement houses or under unsanitary conditions.

Ex-President Roosevelt is equally inaccurate in his criticism of the Jacobs case. He is reported as having said in one of his recent speeches that "the decision of the court in this case retarded by at least twenty years the work of tenement-house reform and was directly responsible for causing hundreds of thousands of American citizens now alive to be brought up under conditions of reeking filth and squalor, which measurably decreased their chance of turning out to be good citizens." The truth is that the decision did not retard tenement-house reform by a single day, and did not prevent the enactment of a single provision for securing sanitary conditions for those who work at home. In fact, the necessary legislation has since been readily secured and enacted in New York without any amendment of the state constitution. Our public health and labor laws now regulate the manufacture of tobacco and other articles in homes and require and secure sanitary conditions, and licenses authorizing manufacturing at home are issued subject to cancellation at any time if the surroundings become unsanitary.

Mr. Sherman characterized as absurd the statement made by Mr. Roosevelt in regard to the effect of this decision, and added that "so far, then, from having done harm in the way of sanitary reform, the decision in the Jacobs case has done good by giving the reform a proper direction and object. Mr. Roosevelt's criticism receives a ready chorus of approval from a large body of ill-informed reformers who seek to prevent some of the evils of 'sweating' by arbitrarily forbidding all home manufacture in tenements. But the vast majority of tenement houses in New York are of a class better described as apartment houses, which are perfectly sanitary, and in such houses there is much home work of a good kind, such as fine sewing, art work, &c., and under good conditions; and it would be a deplorable and unnecessary interference with liberty to forbid such work as an incident to the prevention of home work in unsanitary slums."

Another New York case which is being similarly criticized and misrepresented is what is known as the Bakers case, or People *vs.* Lochner.[1] The decision in this case declaring a statute unconstitutional was that of the Supreme Court of the United States and not of the New York Court of Appeals; in fact the latter court sustained the act, although by a divided court. Mayor Gaynor explained this decision to his audience at Yale, composed largely of law students,

[1] 177 New York Reports, p. 145; 198 United States Reports, p. 45.

in the following language: "The next case in order was the bake-oven case in my state. A bake-oven, you know, is underground. And if any of you ever were in a bake-oven I do not need to say another word about bake-ovens. It is the hottest and most uncomfortable place on the face of the earth. It is a hard place to work in. It is hot and unhealthy, and no one can stand it without injury to health. So in the same way in the state of New York we had an act passed prescribing sanitary regulations for the bakeries. . . . These bake-ovens are exceptional. They are underground and as hot as Tophet, if I may use such an expression here. . . . The law was passed prescribing regulations for them. One of the regulations was that ten hours a night was all that a baker should work in these places." And Mr. Roosevelt is reported in the newspapers as criticizing this decision and stating to his audiences that "this New York law prevented the employment of men in filthy cellar bakeries for longer than ten hours a day."

The statute in question applied to manufacturers of bread, biscuits and confectionery. Taken in connection with the then existing Public Health Law, it contained adequate provisions for securing the best conditions of sanitation and ventilation and for safeguarding bakers from the effects of heat and of breathing flour or other particles. There was no distinction drawn in the act as to hours of labor between sanitary and unsanitary conditions of work, or between bakers and other employees, or between night and day work. The power of the legislature to prevent the manufacture of bread or other articles of food in cellars or in underground bake-ovens or in filthy and unsanitary places, whether above or below ground, was not challenged. The provisions of the act tending to secure sanitary conditions were not interfered with or set aside by the courts, and they have ever since been enforced as valid for all purposes. The act was not confined in its operation to workmen compelled to labor at night underground, but applied to everyone employed day or night in factories, above or below ground, in which bread, confectionery, or biscuits were manufactured. It is true that medical authorities were cited to the courts in support of the view that the trade of a baker was injurious to health, but such authorities were based upon statistics gathered under conditions of labor which could not have existed then and cannot exist now in New York if the elaborate regulations of our public health and labor laws be duly enforced. There were, however, conflicting medical authorities cited to the court, which asserted that the trade was not unwholesome.

Lochner owned a bakery at Utica in which he worked himself and employed three or four workmen. There was only one oven, and it was above ground. The building was clean, especially well ventilated and sanitary. The only question before the court in the case was whether Lochner could be made a criminal and imprisoned for permitting his workmen to labor more than ten hours in any

day under the best sanitary conditions, and the
Supreme Court held that this could not be done
without violating his constitutional rights. Had
the conditions of work in bread, biscuit, or confectionery factories in the state of New York been
shown to have been unusually dangerous and necessarily unwholesome, the law would undoubtedly
have been sustained by the Supreme Court, as was
the Utah miners' act in Holden *vs.* Hardy.[1] No
one who has studied the decisions of the New
York courts or of the Supreme Court of the United
States can doubt that any statutory provision
reasonably tending to protect the health of bakers
and other workmen and to prevent labor in unhealthful places would be upheld as clearly within
the police power of the legislature.

The act, moreover, was one-sided and discriminatory in that it made the employer a criminal but
left the workman free to do as he saw fit. A baker
working for A for ten hours in one day was left
at liberty to go next door to B, A's competitor,
and, if he saw fit, work another ten hours for B.
In fact, as I am told, the informer on whose testimony Lochner was convicted frequently worked ten
hours a day for Lochner and a number of hours
additional in another bakery. If the act had been
honestly conceived in a desire to safeguard the
health of bakers, it would, of course, have provided some punishment for any violation of the
law on the part of the workmen, and not have left

[1] 169 United States Reports, p. 366.

them at liberty to disregard its spirit whenever they saw fit to do so.

The principle involved in this Bakers case was universal, and if employers in bread, biscuit, or confectionery factories could be made criminals for permitting their employees to labor more than ten hours in any one day, the legislature could enact similar legislation as to every other employment. No court would then have power to regulate the degree of the exercise of legislative discretion in such cases. The provision, which at first limited the workday to ten hours, could thereafter be changed to eight hours, or even to six hours, as was advocated in More's "Utopia."

In February of this year, Mr. Roosevelt delivered an address before the Ohio constitutional convention, in which he discussed the decision of the Supreme Court of the United States in the Employers' Liability cases,[1] decided while he was President. The court then held that the act of Congress of June 11, 1906, sometimes erroneously called the National Workmen's Compensation Act, attempted to regulate the internal affairs of the several states as well as interstate commerce, that it consequently included a subject not within the constitutional power of Congress, and that the two matters were so blended that they were incapable of separation unless the court made a new statute in the place of the one enacted by Congress. Conscientiously entertaining this view, the majority of the

[1] 207 United States Reports, p. 463.

court would have been guilty of the plainest constitutional immorality if they had not declared that the act was beyond the power of Congress and declined to give it effect. No honest men, believing as the majority did, could have done otherwise than obey the constitutional mandate expressly reserving to the states the legislative powers not delegated to Congress. In the light of the long-established and wise rule that courts should avoid judicial legislation and not revise or give effect to a statute in a manner not clearly intended by the legislative body, the justices could not, of course, have upheld and enforced the statute simply because the individual cases before them excited their sympathy or involved the claims of widows. The remedy was obvious and simple. Congress was then in session, and within a few days an amended statute could have been enacted so as to limit the act to interstate commerce, which alone was within the constitutional power of Congress to regulate. After the lapse of three months, such a law was enacted, and being plainly confined to interstate commerce, as the original statute should have been, and would have been if properly and competently drafted, the amended act was unanimously sustained by the Supreme Court as constitutional in the Second Employers' Liability cases, decided this year,[1] when it was held that Congress had power to change the common law rules as to assumption of risk, contributory negligence and fellow-servants' acts in

[1] 223 United States Reports, p. 1.

connection with the regulation of interstate commerce.

Speaking of the first decision, Mr. Roosevelt said: "When I was President, we passed a National Workmen's Compensation Act. Under it a railway man named Howard, I think, was killed in Tennessee, and his widow sued for damages. Congress had done all it could to provide the right, but the court stepped in and decreed that Congress had failed. Three of the judges took the extreme position that there was no way in which Congress could act to secure the helpless widow and children against suffering, and that the man's blood and the blood of all similar men when spilled should forever cry aloud in vain for justice. This seems a strong statement, but it is far less strong than the actual facts; and I have difficulty in making the statement with any degree of moderation. The nine justices of the Supreme Court on this question split into five fragments. One man, Justice Moody, in his opinion stated the case in its broadest way and demanded justice for Howard, on grounds that would have meant that in all similar cases thereafter justice and not injustice should be done. Yet the court, by a majority of one, decided as I do not for one moment believe the court would now decide, and not only perpetuated a lamentable injustice in the case of the man himself, but set a standard of injustice for all similar cases. Here again I ask you not to think of mere legal formalism, but to think of the great immutable principles of jus-

tice, the great immutable principles of right and
wrong, and to ponder what it means to men dependent for their livelihood, and to the women and
children dependent upon these men, when the courts
of the land deny them the justice to which they are
entitled."

Now, if this argument meant anything it certainly
meant that, in the opinion of the speaker, an ex-
President of the United States, the justices of the
Supreme Court should have disregarded the Constitution as they understood it in order to allow a
widow to recover notwithstanding the unconstitu-
tionality of the act under and by virtue of which
she was suing. You will not find a single word of
reference by Mr. Roosevelt in his whole address
to the only point upon which the majority, speaking
by Mr. Justice White, decided the cases. Of course,
the statement of what was actually decided would
have been tame and unsensational. The criticism
in form and substance was based upon a distorted
and unfair statement of what was decided, and it
was calculated to create in the minds of the members of the Ohio constitutional convention, as well
as in the minds of the uninformed public, the
belief that the justices of the Supreme Court of
the United States had "set a standard of injustice
for all similar cases" and had denied to Congress
the power to pass a fair and just employers' liability
statute properly limited to interstate commerce.
The contrary was plainly the truth, as the subsequent decision of the court had clearly shown, for

this latter decision was rendered and published before Mr. Roosevelt made his address.

Another example of distorted statement and unfair criticism of the courts will be found in the same address. It related to the decision of the New York Court of Appeals in the case of Ives *vs.* South Buffalo Railway Company,[1] decided last year, in which the court held that a statute concededly novel and revolutionary, creating liability on the part of an employer to his workmen although the employer and his agents were wholly free from negligence or fault of any kind and had neglected no duty of care, supervision or selection, was unconstitutional because taking the property of the employer and giving it to the workman without due process of law. Ives was a brakeman employed by the defendant railway company. While walking on the top of the cars of a very long train, he gave a signal to the engineer to close up a space or slack and was thrown to the ground by the resulting jar, concededly without any negligence on the part of the railway company, and probably through his own carelessness. The injury consisted of a sprained ankle and slight bruises. There was no claim in the complaint that the injury was in any sense permanent, and as matter of fact Ives sued for loss of wages during only five weeks, claiming fifty dollars as the measure of his damage. I am informed that the injury was not serious, that Ives entirely recovered and resumed his work within

[1] 201 New York Reports, p. 271.

four weeks after the injury, that the railroad company ultimately paid him for his loss of time, that he has since been continuously employed by the same company at similar work, and that in no sense whatever was his ability to earn his livelihood impaired.

Let us turn to the picture drawn by Mr. Roosevelt in describing this case for the instruction and guidance of a constitutional convention. "I am not thinking of the terminology of the decision, nor of what seem to me the hair-splitting and meticulous arguments elaborately worked out to justify a great and terrible miscarriage of justice. Moreover, I am not thinking only of the sufferers in any given case, but of the tens of thousands of others who suffer because of the way this case was decided. In the New York case, the railway employee who was injured was a man named, I believe, Ives. The court admits that by every moral consideration he was entitled to recover as his due the money that the law intended to give him. Yet the court by its decision forces that man to stagger through life maimed, and keeps the money that should be his in the treasury of the company in whose service, as an incident of his regular employment and in the endurance of ordinary risks, he lost the ability to earn his own livelihood. There are thousands of Iveses in this country; thousands of cases such as this come up every year; and while this is true, while the courts deny essential and elementary justice to these men and give to them and the people in exchange for justice a technical and empty formula, it is idle to ask me not to criticize them. As long as injustice is kept thus intrenched by any court, I will protest as strongly as in me lies against such action."

To repeat, as a matter of fact, Ives was not maimed; he was not permanently injured; he was not deprived of the ability to earn his livelihood. Nor did the Court of Appeals admit that by every moral consideration Ives was entitled to recover as his due the money that the law intended to give him. Had that point been before a court of justice, however sympathetic and sentimental, I doubt very much whether it could have held that Ives was entitled, by any moral consideration whatever, to compel the railway company to compensate him for the four or five weeks' loss of wages resulting from no fault on its part but from his own carelessness. The statements that "the court by its decision forces that man to stagger through life maimed" and that "he lost the ability to earn his own livelihood" were simply so much fiction, but, of course they were very effective with emotional audiences and highly calculated to inflame Mr. Roosevelt's hearers and readers against the courts. I venture to assert that it would be difficult to find or indeed to conceive a more unwarranted and unfair misrepresentation of the facts actually before a court.

Another current misrepresentation is that the Supreme Court of the United States in the Second Employers' Liability cases upheld as constitutional a statute of Congress identical with the statute held unconstitutional by the New York Court of Appeals in the Ives case. The people are being told that the New York courts hold the provision requiring due process of law in the fourteenth amendment to mean one thing, whilst the Supreme Court of the United States holds exactly the same provision in the fifth amendment to mean the contrary. But those who will take the trouble to read the two statutes will at once perceive that the act of Congress differs radically from the New York Workmen's Compensation Act. The act of Congress, although abolishing or restricting the rules as to fellow-servants' acts, assumption of risk and contributory negligence, imposes liability on common carriers by railroad only for "injury or death resulting in whole or in part from the *negligence* of any of the officers, agents, or employees of such carrier, or by reason of any defect or insufficiency, *due to its negligence*, in its cars, engines, appliances, machinery, track, roadbed, works, boats, wharves, or other equipment." On the other hand, the New York statute created liability not in one dangerous employment, such as the business of common carrier by railroad, but in many other employments not necessarily dangerous, and wholly irrespective of negligence or fault on the part of the employer or any of his officers, agents, or employees. In fact, there is nothing in the New York decision or in the opinions of the judges which would invalidate a statute identical with the act of Congress if now enacted by the New York legislature. The Ives case, far from preventing such a statute, would be an authority in its support.

I regret that we have not time to consider further these particular decisions. In my opinion they correctly and wisely applied established principles of constitutional law and constitutional justice and were morally right and just. I am now pleading for fairness and temperance in discussing the decisions of our courts and for the imperative necessity of founding these discussions upon the truth. Ambassador Bryce said in a recent address: "To counsel you to stick to facts is not to dissuade you from philosophical generalizations, but only to remind you . . . that the generalizations must spring out of the facts, and without the facts are worthless." In other words, a regard for fact, which is but another term for truth, is or should be as indispensable in law and politics as it is in philosophy.

The criticisms of which the above are fair samples must be refuted because they find constant repetition and have the authority of distinguished leaders of public opinion, who at the present time seem to have the confidence of the people. Their statements are naturally accepted as true. The judges are being similarly misrepresented and assailed on all sides, and they cannot defend themselves. Thus far the bar at large has seemed indifferent, and a misconception of what constitutes good taste imposes silence upon the counsel engaged in the cases which are criticized. The people are being

misled, prejudiced and inflamed by false statements
and unfair criticism.   If the courts are not defended,
they may bend before the storm of undeserved
censure.   Constituted as humanity is, there is grave
danger that the judges will be unconsciously intimidated and coerced by this abuse and clamor.
Is it not high time that the members of our profession should charge themselves with the task of
defending the courts by placing the facts before the
people?   The bar associations of the country will
never be called upon to render a greater service
to the profession and to the community than that
of stemming this tide of misrepresentation and
intemperate abuse and striving to restore confidence
in the learning, impartiality and independence of
our judges, in the justice of their decisions, and
in the necessity of their enforcing constitutional
restraints.

Not only are the decisions of the courts constantly
distorted and misrepresented, but the people are
also being taught that the courts have usurped the
power to declare void any statute in conflict with
the constitution, and that no such power was ever
intended to be conferred by the framers of national
or state constitutions.   Surely by this time it ought
to be manifest that if the courts may not adjudge
invalid and refuse to give force and effect to unconstitutional enactments, it is of little or no use to
declare in constitutions that legislatures shall not
pass bills of attainder, or ex post facto laws, or laws
abridging the freedom of speech, or of the press, or

prohibiting the free exercise of religion, or denying the right to trial by jury, or imprisoning without trial, or suspending the writ of habeas corpus, or confiscating private property.

Speaking on this subject of judicial power and duty, Hamilton in the "Federalist" used language which cannot be too often repeated. He clearly showed that in 1788 it was understood and contemplated that the courts should exercise the power to adjudge invalid any statute which was in conflict with the Constitution. In fact, such power had then already been exercised by state courts. He said that constitutional limitations "can be preserved in practice no other way than through the medium of courts of justice, whose duty it must be to declare all acts contrary to the manifest tenor of the Constitution void. Without this, all the reservation of particular rights or privileges would amount to nothing. . . . There is no position which depends on clearer principles than that every act of a delegated authority, contrary to the tenor of the commission under which it is exercised, is void. No legislative act, therefore, contrary to the Constitution, can be valid. To deny this would be to affirm that the deputy is greater than his principal; that the servant is above his master; that the representatives of the people are superior to the people themselves; that men acting by virtue of powers may do not only what their powers do not authorize, but what they forbid. . . . The interpretation of the laws is the proper and peculiar province of the courts. A constitution is, in fact, and must be regarded by the judges, as a fundamental law. It therefore belongs to them to ascertain its meaning, as well as the meaning of any particular act proceeding from the legislative body. If there should happen to be an irreconcilable variance between the two, that which has the superior obligation and validity ought, of course, to be preferred; or, in other words, the Constitution ought to be preferred to the statute; the intention of the people to the intention of their agents. Nor does this conclusion by any means suppose a superiority of the judicial to the legislative power. It only supposes that the power of the people is superior to both; and that where the will of the legislature, declared in its statutes, stands in opposition to that of the people, declared in the Constitution, the judges ought to be governed by the latter rather than the former. They ought to regulate their decisions by the fundamental laws, rather than by those which are not fundamental." [1]

Equally conclusive and equally worthy of constant repetition is the reasoning of Chief Justice Marshall in Marbury *vs.* Madison, where he said: "To what purpose are powers limited, and to what purpose is that limitation committed to writing, if these limitations may, at any time, be passed by those intended to be restrained? The distinction between a government with limited and unlimited powers is abolished, if those limits do not confine the persons on whom

---

[1] The Federalist, Ford's edition, pp. 520, 521, 522.

they are imposed, and if acts prohibited and acts allowed are of equal obligation. It is a proposition too plain to be contested, that the Constitution controls any legislative act repugnant to it; or, that the legislature may alter the Constitution by an ordinary act. Between these alternatives there is no middle ground. The Constitution is either a superior paramount law, unchangeable by ordinary means, or it is on a level with ordinary legislative acts, and, like other acts, is alterable when the legislature shall please to alter it. If the former part of the alternative be true, then a legislative act contrary to the Constitution is not law: if the latter part be true, then written constitutions are absurd attempts, on the part of the people, to limit a power in its own nature illimitable." [1]

This decision of the Supreme Court to the effect that it is the duty and within the power of the courts to construe constitutions and to refuse to enforce unconstitutional enactments was rendered in 1803. Yet, notwithstanding that the Constitution of the United States has been amended four times since that decision, and that every state constitution has been again and again remodeled or amended, no American constitution has ever denied to the courts the power to construe constitutions or the duty to refuse to enforce statutes which are in conflict with constitutional limitations. If the power to declare void any statute in conflict with the Constitution of the United States was deemed necessary

[1] 1 Cranch's Reports, pp. 176–177.

in 1788 when Hamilton was writing his famous
essays, it certainly ought to be far more necessary
in our day of multiform legislation, vast increase in
the functions of the state, and incompetent, reckless
and oppressive class legislation interfering in almost
every conceivable manner with the rights and
liberties of the individual.

Moreover, the Constitution of the United States
would probably never have been adopted if the
people had understood, as is now pretended, that
Congress was to be at liberty to disregard constitutional limitations and guaranties and that there
would be no way whatever of preventing a violation
by Congress of the constitutional rights of the
individual except at the polls. All students of our
history know that the Constitution was accepted
by the people upon the distinct pledge that amendments embodying a bill of rights to protect the
individual against Congress would be immediately
adopted. And one of the first acts of the First
Congress in September, 1789, was to submit the
ten amendments known as the federal bill of
rights, which were thereupon ratified by the states
and became an integral part of the Constitution.
But of what avail or benefit were these amendments if Congress was not to be effectively restrained
and bound by them? It is no exaggeration to say
that if the courts should now be deprived of the
power to protect litigants who invoke constitutional
guaranties and should be compelled to enforce, as
valid laws, statutes which violate the limitations

upon legislative power which the people have deliberately embodied in their fundamental law, our
constitutions would become dead letters, and we
might as well turn to the pure and unrestrained
democracy of Greece and await her fate.

In an inspiring address delivered this year before
the New York State Bar Association on the subject
of judicial decisions and public feeling, Senator
Root eloquently said: "A sovereign people which
declares that all men have certain inalienable rights,
and imposes upon itself the great impersonal rules
of conduct deemed necessary for the preservation
of those rights, and at the same time declares that
it will disregard those rules whenever, in any particular case, it is the wish of a majority of its voters to
do so, establishes as complete a contradiction to
the fundamental principles of our government as it
is possible to conceive. It abandons absolutely
the conception of a justice which is above majorities,
of a right in the weak which the strong are bound to
respect. It denies the vital truth taught by religion
and realized in the hard experience of mankind, and
which has inspired every constitution America has
produced and every great declaration for human
freedom since Magna Carta — the truth that
human nature needs to distrust its own impulses
and passions, and to establish for its own control
the restraining and guiding influence of declared
principles of action."

In many of the current assaults upon the judicial
department, in support often of schemes having

their birthplace on the continent of Europe, we find the complaint that in declaring statutes unconstitutional the courts in this country — state and federal — exercise greater power than the courts of other countries are authorized to exercise. As if that were an argument against American institutions! Every schoolboy knows that the framers intended that our government should differ from every other government in the world. The founders not only intentionally departed from the examples of existing governments, but anxiously sought to establish a new form of republican government, which would perpetuate the spirit of the Declaration of Independence, secure the inalienable rights of the individual, and protect the minority against the oppression or tyranny of the majority. It was because these rights of the individual against majorities and every form of governmental power were to be made secure and sacred, as the founders believed, that we were to differ from other governments. And the essential and effective feature of that difference was to lie in the power vested in the judicial department to uphold and protect these rights. High sounding declarations of the rights of man would mean very little if they were not to be enforceable by the courts.

When our form of government is compared with that of other countries, and we are told that in England or in France or elsewhere so-called progressive measures have been forced into immediate operation by the will of the majority, and that the

ess to interfere, is it seri-
to the people of the United
, therefore, cast aside all
all their ancient and honest
, and leave the protection
rty wholly in the hands of
Are there not still certain
who are assailing our institu-
ion of the very Constitution
t to have protected by our
ged that the courts should
are an act unconstitutional,
but should be compelled to enforce all legislative
enactments although some of them might conflict
with the Constitution, is it realized that the bill of
rights would then be left to the arbitrary discretion
or caprice of the legislature, and that consequently
it would be of no more practical protection to the
individual than the paper constitutions of some of
the South American republics which, too, contain
eloquent declarations of the rights of the individual?
Is it forgotten or overlooked that in England and
France and all the other countries with whose
systems of government ours is being compared,
the legislative power is practically supreme, and
that it can outlaw or disseize or imprison at its
mere will — that it can deny religious liberty,
abridge the freedom of speech or of the press, pass
bills of attainder and ex post facto laws, suspend the
writ of habeas corpus, impose cruel and unusual pun-
ishments, deny to the individual accused of crime the

right to a jury-trial or even any hearing at all, confiscate private property without compensation, and impair the obligation of contracts?

Let us, for example, suppose that Congress or a state legislature saw fit to imprison those who did not profess the religion of the majority, or observe its forms and tenets. Who could then protect the minority against such tyrannical enactments except the courts, and how could the courts shield them save by declaring the statute unconstitutional and void and refusing to enforce it? We have only to go back a few generations to find just such laws in England and in the American colonies, and it is the repetition of them that our constitutions seek to prevent. Suppose again that Congress or a state legislature should pass a statute abridging the freedom of speech or of the press and making those who violated the statute subject to criminal prosecution and imprisonment. How could the individual be then protected except by the judiciary, and how could the judiciary protect him unless by exercising the power to declare the statute unconstitutional?

Do the agitators who are attacking our constitutional system explain to their listeners that in the foreign governments with which they are making comparisons the legislative power could compel workmen in any trade to work as many hours a day, at such rates of wages, and under such conditions as the majority saw fit to enact? Suppose that the Pennsylvania legislature should pass a statute compelling laborers in coal mines to labor twelve or more hours a day for a compensation fixed by it and providing that refusal should constitute a crime. Or similarly in the case of railroad employees. In doing so, the legislature would find a precedent in the famous English Statute of Labourers as well as in numerous other European enactments. The Pennsylvania legislature might pass an act, similar to that enacted by the British parliament in 1720 and again in 1800, making it a crime for laborers to combine to obtain an advance of wages or to lessen or alter their hours of work. Is it inconceivable that the time may come when the majority of the voters in Pennsylvania will believe that it is imperative thus to regulate labor in coal mines and on the railroads, both of which industries are indispensable, serve every household in the state, affect every individual, rich or poor, and compel all to pay tribute? Might not prejudice and self-interest tempt or impel to such a statute, and might not the majority enact it, particularly if those affected were aliens without political power? Is it inconceivable that the owners of the coal mines and the railroads may some day control a majority in the legislature? But how could these miners and railroad employees be protected from such enactments and criminal prosecutions thereunder unless the courts had the power to declare statutes unconstitutional and to refuse to enforce them because depriving the individual of his constitutional rights?

In nine cases out of ten the answer to these suggestions by those who to-day are assailing the judicial

department would undoubtedly be that no one
intends to go to any such extreme, and that no one
wishes to be placed or to place any one else entirely
at the mercy of the legislature. Thus, they would
concede that some rights should still be safeguarded
by the courts. But does not this answer contain
the gist of the whole problem and the whole principle and virtue of the American system of constitutional restraints? If the critics of our system
would have some rights, and particularly their own,
protected by the courts, must they not then confess
that in truth they only wish changes where the
rights of others are concerned, and that they would
cling to the Constitution and invoke the protection
of the judicial power in all those respects in which
their own personal liberty and their own personal
and property rights are affected? Chief Judge Cullen of the New York Court of Appeals recently said
that "the great misfortune of the day is the mania
for regulating all human conduct by statute, from
responsibility for which few are exempt, since many
of our most intelligent and highly educated citizens,
who resent as paternalism and socialism legislative
interference with affairs in which they are interested, are most persistent in the attempt to regulate
by law the conduct of others." [1]

I do not doubt that if we could have an exhaustive
debate before a great tribunal of American public
opinion and could step by step analyze and sift the
arguments against the judicial power in constitu-

[1] 204 New York Reports, p. 534.

tional cases, we would find in the final analysis that those who are so fiercely charging the courts with usurping power by refusing to enforce unconstitutional enactments would still want the continued protection of the courts so far as their own constitutional rights and liberties were concerned, and that they were only asking modification and curtailment in respect of the rights and liberties of others. I am confident that if it were left to the people of the United States to determine by their votes the simple question whether they would place in the hands of Congress or of their state legislatures the fundamental, elemental, inalienable rights which every American citizen now enjoys — the inalienable rights proclaimed in the Declaration of Independence — an overwhelming vote would be cast against any such change. Indeed, support for this conviction may be found in the recent experience of Australia, that hotbed of radicalism. An attempt by constitutional amendment to curtail the power of the judiciary in labor controversies and to confer upon the Australian parliament all power necessary to deal with labor matters was there the subject of a referendum and met with a decisive defeat at the polls. Are we likely to be less conservative than the Australians, or to be less mindful of the necessity for wise constitutional guaranties and restraints?

The truth is that our constitutions, national and state, do not stand in the way of any fair and just exercise of what is called the police power, or of measures for social progress or social justice, and that they do not prevent reasonable and just regulations tending to secure the health and promote the welfare of the community at large, or the enactment of proper and reasonable factory laws or proper and reasonable workmen's compensation acts. The main source of trouble is that the statutes which the courts are compelled to refuse to enforce are very often hastily and crudely drawn, and are often inherently unreasonable and unjust.

But, even if this be not so; even if the people, after full statement of the facts and thorough explanation of the effect of the change, upon mature consideration desire to vest greater power in our legislatures, or to curtail the power of the courts, the means are within their reach. In New York and in other states, the Constitution can be easily amended within two years.

It has been repeatedly asserted that the Constitution of the United States has become practically unamendable, when as a matter of fact its amendment does not involve any greater difficulties than were intended or than would seem reasonably necessary, or than would be provided if we were now framing a new national constitution. The prescribed machinery of a vote by two-thirds of both houses of Congress and ratification by three-fourths of the states simply compels deliberation and prevents hasty and unconsidered action. If the people of the country really desire a particular amendment to the Constitution of the United States, it ought to be readily obtainable within less than two years.

Thus, the first ten amendments were proposed by Congress in September, 1789, and were adopted in those days of slow travel and difficult communication by eight states within six months and by the requisite three-fourths within two years. The twelfth amendment, proposed in 1803, was ratified in nine months. The thirteenth amendment, proposed by Congress in 1865, was ratified by the legislatures of twenty-seven out of the then thirty-six states within ten months; and the fifteenth amendment, the latest, proposed in February, 1869, was ratified by twenty-nine out of the thirty-seven states within one year. The delay in the adoption of the proposed sixteenth amendment authorizing Congress to levy an income tax is due wholly to the fact that there is a serious difference of opinion as to whether or not this power should be conferred, although the advocates of the amendment confidently proclaimed the existence of an almost universal desire on the part of the people for such an amendment to the Constitution.[1]

One of the most insidious suggestions that can possibly be made to the people at large is that there is an insurmountable difficulty in securing amendments to our constitutions, just as misleading and dangerous as it is for them to be told that their

---

[1] Since this address was delivered, the sixteenth amendment has been ratified. It was proposed by Congress July 16, 1909, and declared effective February 25, 1913. The seventeenth amendment was proposed by Congress May 15, 1912, and declared effective May 31, 1913. In view of this demonstration, it should certainly not be any longer urged that the Constitution of the United States is practically unamendable.

desires are being thwarted by the judiciary and that they must accomplish reforms either by coercing the courts or by undermining the foundations of their constitutions. The future contentment of the people requires that they shall feel that the governments, state and federal, are their governments, that they themselves are ultimately the sovereign power, and that they are at liberty to amend the organic law from time to time as their mature and deliberate judgment shall deem necessary or desirable. All that the conservatives can ask or do ask is that the people shall act deliberately and under circumstances calculated to afford time and opportunity for full explanation and a full understanding of the scope and tendency of the proposed changes, to the end that errors may be discovered and exposed, that theorizing, sentimentalism, clamor and prejudice may exhaust themselves, and that the sober second thought of every part of the country may be asserted. If it be then determined to amend our constitutions, even to the extent of placing life, liberty and property at the unrestrained discretion and mercy of our legislators, the will of the sovereign people will have to be obeyed. Let us hope and pray, however, that when amendments are adopted, they will be conservative and wise, that the rights of the minority as against the majority will not be heedlessly sacrificed for the temporary advantage of one class over another, and that it will be appreciated that individual liberty should be the vital concern of every man, rich or poor, as

being essential to the perpetuation of the institutions which we cherish as peculiarly and preemi-
nently American.   Let us especially try to avoid
permitting any class to make use of constitutional
amendments or of statutory enactments for its own
special purposes.   Let us, whilst meeting in full
sympathy, generosity and charity the legitimate
demands of the laboring classes and of the poor and
humble, nevertheless keep our eyes open to prevent
any such vicious results as would arise from constitutional or statutory provisions framed nominally
for the benefit of labor but really for the purpose of
serving the interests of a particular class against
another, as we have seen was the case in the New
York tenement-house legislation of 1884.   In the
meantime, pending such amendments in the due,
orderly and reasonable course prescribed by our
constitutions, let us be faithful and devoted to our
constitutional system, which for more than a century has carried us through every storm and so often
"in spite of false lights on the shore."   Let us also
be truthful and fair and, if possible, temperate in
our criticism of all public officials, whether legislative, executive, or judicial.

Finally, a word about the special duty of our
profession.   It is not the pulpit nor the press, but
the law which reaches and touches every fibre of
the whole fabric of life, which surrounds and guards
every right of the individual, which grasps the
greatest and the least of human affairs, and which
comprehends the whole community and every human

right. We lawyers, if worthy of our profession, are
in duty bound not merely to defend constitutional
guaranties before the courts for individual clients,
but to teach the people in season and out of season
to value and respect the constitutional rights of
others and to respect and cherish the institutions
which we have inherited. It is our duty to preach
constitutional morality to the rich and to the poor,
to all trades and to all professions, to all ranks and
to all classes, in the cities and on the plains. It is
for us to convince the members of every class that,
in the long run, disregard of the fundamental rights
of others would be in conflict with their own permanent welfare and happiness, and cannot be permitted
if we are to remain a free people. What higher duty,
what nobler task could engage us than to teach
the value and sacredness of the ancient and honest
principles of justice embodied in our constitutions, immortal as the eternal truths from which
they derive their origin, and to preach to all classes
the virtue of political justice and self-imposed political restraints, without which there can be no true
constitutional morality.

THE ELEVENTH AMENDMENT [1]

O F the important questions of constitutional law now before the country, none more vitally affects the peace and harmony of our dual system of government than that of the power of a federal court to enjoin a state officer from enforcing the provisions of a state statute which is in conflict with the Constitution of the United States. This question usually arises in connection with the eleventh article of amendment, which provides that "the judicial power of the United States shall not be construed to extend to any suit in law or equity, commenced or prosecuted against one of the United States by citizens of another state, or by citizens or subjects of any foreign state." Serious controversies regarding the issuance of injunctions by federal courts against state officers have arisen in New York, North Carolina, Alabama, Missouri, Kansas, Minnesota, and other states. A convention of attorneys-general from a number of states, held at St. Louis in September and October, 1907, adopted a memorial to the President and Congress praying that the jurisdiction of the circuit courts of the United States might be curtailed in respect of suits brought to

[1] Address before the New York State Bar Association at its thirty-first annual meeting held in New York, January 25, 1908.

restrain state officers from enforcing state laws or the orders of state administrative boards. The President in his annual message to Congress called the matter to the attention of that body, and stated that discontent was often expressed with the use of the process of injunction by the courts where state laws were concerned. The assembling of Congress was marked by the introduction of numerous bills to curtail the power of the federal courts to issue injunctions and by the offering of several joint resolutions to amend the Constitution of the United States, which had the same object. The question will, perhaps, figure prominently in the next presidential campaign. It may, therefore, be appropriate to review at this time the history of the eleventh article of amendment to the Constitution of the United States in order to see what light that history throws upon the purpose of its framers. Did they intend, in prohibiting suits by an individual against a state, to deny to the courts of the United States the power to enjoin a state officer from enforcing a state statute in conflict with the Constitution of the United States?

In 1787 and 1788, when the adoption of the Constitution was under consideration by the people of the United States, conflicting views were entertained as to the suability of a state by an individual for the recovery of claims against it. Hamilton, Madison and Marshall expressed the opinion that a state would not be suable by an individual under the Constitution as drafted. A number of prominent men, conspicuous among whom were Edmund Pendleton, Patrick Henry and George Mason, were of opinion that the language of the judicial clause conferred jurisdiction to entertain and determine such a suit. Some urged this as an objection to the Constitution. Others, including James Wilson of Pennsylvania and Edmund Randolph of Virginia, two of the most distinguished lawyers and publicists of the day and members of the Constitutional Convention, contended not only that jurisdiction was conferred but that it was wise and necessary that such jurisdiction should exist. Wilson urged that "when a citizen has a controversy with another state, there ought to be a tribunal where both parties may stand on a just and equal footing," and Randolph argued that the jurisdiction would tend "to render valid and effective existing claims, and secure that justice, ultimately, which is to be found in every regular government." The Constitution of the United States was adopted as submitted with the understanding that amendments would be promptly proposed. The First Congress submitted twelve amendments, ten of which were adopted, but the suability of a state was not mentioned in any of them.

The question was presented for judicial decision in 1792 in an action brought by Chisholm, a citizen of the state of South Carolina, against the state of Georgia in the Supreme Court of the United States under its original jurisdiction.[1] The action was in assumpsit to recover a debt. The court then consisted of Chief

[1] 2 Dallas' Reports, p. 419.

Justice Jay and Justices Cushing, Wilson, Blair, Johnson and Iredell. On February 18, 1793, the court held, Mr. Justice Iredell alone dissenting, that under the Constitution as originally adopted a state could be sued in that court by a citizen of another state in an action of assumpsit to enforce the payment of a contract debt. This decision, which was followed by the commencement of the suit of Vassal *vs.* Massachusetts, created irritation and alarm among the states, and particularly among those which were heavily burdened with debt. The anti-Federalist prints were loud in invectives against the decision, which was termed a violation of the sovereignty of the states, and it was declared that the people were "called upon to draw their swords against this invasion of their rights." It has been said, though with some exaggeration, that "the states fairly rose in rebellion against the decision." Four states formally protested. Although Georgia had been the first state to invoke the original jurisdiction of the Supreme Court, it nevertheless refused to appear in the Chisholm suit, and filed a remonstrance and protestation against the exercise of jurisdiction. After the decision, it openly defied the authority of the national judiciary. Indeed, it is stated by McMaster, Cooley and other writers that the legislature of Georgia at once passed a law subjecting to death without benefit of clergy any officer who should attempt to serve a process in any suit against the state, but no record of any such statute can be found. Probably, as some one has suggested, the supposed law was a bill which passed only the lower branch of the legislature. At all events, the legislatures of Virginia, Massachusetts and Connecticut instructed their senators and representatives to secure the adoption of an amendment to the Constitution which should prevent suits against a state by an individual.

On February 20, 1793, two days after the opinions in Chisholm *vs.* Georgia were delivered, a resolution was offered in the United States Senate proposing an amendment of the Constitution in the following terms: "The judicial power of the United States shall not extend to any suits in law or equity, commenced or prosecuted against one of the United States by citizens of another state or by citizens or subjects of any foreign state."

The proposed amendment was debated to some extent in the Second Congress, but it was not passed. In the Third Congress, on January 2, 1794, Caleb Strong, one of the senators from Massachusetts, moved the adoption of a resolution which changed the form of the proposed amendment so as to read as follows: "The judicial power of the United States shall not *be construed to* extend to any suit in law or equity, commenced or prosecuted against one of the United States by citizens of another state, or by citizens or subjects of any foreign state."

The amendment was finally accepted in this form on March 4, 1794, and was at once submitted to the legislatures of the several states for ratification, but up to March, 1797, there were still eight states

which had not acted upon it, probably because the
political clamor had subsided, and there was no longer
any demand for amendment.   In fact, Congress had
to request the President to communicate with the
outstanding states upon the subject.   Finally, in a
message from President Adams to Congress dated
January 8, 1798, the proposed amendment was declared to have been ratified by three-fourths of the
states, and it thereupon became the eleventh article
of amendment to the Constitution of the United
States.   New Jersey and Pennsylvania had refused
to ratify it, while South Carolina and Tennessee had
taken no action.

The unusual and peculiar wording of the amendment first attracts attention.   Instead of declaring
how the Constitution shall read in the future, it
declares how it shall "not be construed."   This
phraseology was used for political reasons and as a
concession to the susceptibilities of the advocates of
state rights.   Extremists wanted a declaration that
would not only overrule the recent construction of
the Constitution by the Supreme Court and deny
that such a power had ever existed, but would also
oust all jurisdiction in pending as well as in future
cases.   The amendment, therefore, does not purport
to amend or alter the Constitution, but to maintain
it unchanged, while controlling its scope and effect
by authoritatively declaring how it shall not be
construed.

Speaking of the language of the amendment,
Chief Justice Marshall said in the case of Cohens

vs. Virginia: "It is a part of our history, that, at the adoption of the Constitution, all the states were greatly indebted; and the apprehension that these debts might be prosecuted in the federal courts formed a very serious objection to that instrument. Suits were instituted, and the court maintained its jurisdiction. The alarm was general; and, to quiet the apprehensions that were so extensively entertained, this amendment was proposed in Congress, and adopted by the state legislatures. That its motive was not to maintain the sovereignty of a state from the degradation supposed to attend a compulsory appearance before the tribunal of the nation, may be inferred from the terms of the amendment. It does not comprehend controversies between two or more states, or between a state and a foreign state. The jurisdiction of the court still extends to these cases: and in these a state may still be sued. We must ascribe the amendment, then, to some other cause than the dignity of a state. There is no difficulty in finding this cause. Those who were inhibited from commencing a suit against a state, or from prosecuting one which might be commenced before the adoption of the amendment, were persons who might probably be its creditors. There was not much reason to fear that foreign or sister states would be creditors to any considerable amount, and there was reason to retain the jurisdiction of the court in those cases, because it might be essential to the preservation of peace. The amendment, therefore, extended to suits commenced or prosecuted by individuals, but not to those brought by states.

"The first impression made on the mind by this amendment is, that it was intended for those cases, and for those only, in which some demand against a state is made by an individual in the courts of the Union. If we consider the causes to which it is to be traced, we are conducted to the same conclusion. A general interest might well be felt in leaving to a state the full power of consulting its convenience in the adjustment of its debts or of other claims upon it; but no interest could be felt in so changing the relations between the whole and its parts, as to strip the government of the means of protecting, by the instrumentality of its courts, the Constitution and laws from active violation."[1]

It will also be observed that the amendment does not refer to suits against a state by one of its own citizens. This was undoubtedly because the Constitution did not extend the judicial power of the United States, when dependent upon the character of the parties, to controversies between a state and its own citizens, but only to controversies between a state and citizens of another state or citizens or subjects of foreign states. The distinction between jurisdiction dependent upon the nature or subject matter of the controversy irrespective of the character of the parties, such as cases arising under the Constitution, laws and treaties of the United States, and jurisdiction dependent upon the character of

[1] 6 Wheaton's Reports, pp. 406–407.

the parties irrespective of the nature or subject matter of the controversy, had probably not then been as clearly recognized as was subsequently done by Chief Justice Marshall. The failure of the eleventh amendment to mention suits against a state by its own citizens gave rise nearly one hundred years later to the contention that a state could be sued in a circuit court of the United States by one of its own citizens in a case arising under the Constitution. This was urged at the October term, 1889, in Hans vs. Louisiana and North Carolina vs. Temple,[1] but the court overruled the contention and held that a state could not be sued by an individual in a United States court even in a case arising under the Constitution. Mr. Justice Bradley delivered the opinion of the court. He criticized the reasoning of the majority in Chisholm vs. Georgia, and upheld the dissenting opinion of Mr. Justice Iredell to the effect that, under the Constitution as originally adopted, no suit could be maintained against a state by an individual to enforce its debts except by its consent. Mr. Justice Harlan, however, while he concurred in holding that a suit directly against a state by one of its own citizens to enforce a debt was not within the judicial power of the United States, criticized the comments made by Mr. Justice Bradley upon the decision in Chisholm vs. Georgia as not necessary to the determination of the case, and expressed the opinion that the prior decision was based upon a sound inter-

[1] 134 United States Reports, pp. 1, 22.

pretation of the Constitution as that instrument was then worded.

It has been stated in opinions of the Supreme Court that a state can be sued in a court of the United States by an individual if it waives its immunity and consents to be sued. But it is difficult to perceive how the consent or waiver of a state can, in any case and under any circumstances, confer upon the federal courts jurisdiction of a suit against it by a citizen of another state or a citizen or subject of a foreign state in the face of the imperative mandate of the amendment that "the judicial power of the United States shall *not be construed to extend* to" any such suit. It is true that the court in the case of Clark *vs.* Barnard said that the immunity of a state from suit in a federal court was a personal privilege which it might waive at pleasure and that its appearance as a party defendant in a court of the United States would be a voluntary submission to its jurisdiction,[1] but in that case the state intervened as an actor and its intervention was such that it could be treated substantially as a plaintiff and the jurisdiction sustained on the ground that a state may sue an individual in a federal court. Although in the more recent case of Gunter *vs.* Atlantic Coast Line,[2] Mr. Justice White, delivering the opinion of the court, declared it to be an elementary proposition that a state could waive its immunity, it will be observed that in that case

[1] 108 United States Reports, p. 447.
[2] 200 United States Reports, pp. 283, 284.

the suit was in fact against an officer of the state
of South Carolina, and that the state itself was
not a party to the record. It seems to me, with
all deference, that the court has not yet squarely
passed upon the point, nor, so far as I know, has
it ever questioned the fundamental principle that
a federal court cannot exercise jurisdiction in any
case to which the judicial power of the United
States, as delegated and defined in the Constitution,
does not extend. An entirely different question is
presented when we consider whether an officer of
a state can consent or be authorized to consent to
be sued in a federal court; in other words, whether
he can waive the defense that the state is a
necessary party to the suit. It does not follow that,
because a state cannot be sued, it may not authorize
its agent to defend on the merits without pleading
the absence of the state as the real party in interest,
and the denial of jurisdiction over the state as
principal does not necessarily imply a denial of
jurisdiction over the officer when doing or attempt-
ing to do an illegal act as its agent or representative. So, also, a different question is presented
under the later amendments, which may be held to
have qualified the eleventh amendment in authorizing Congress to enforce their provisions by appropriate legislation. As to that point I am not now
prepared to express an opinion.

In construing the eleventh amendment for the
purpose of ascertaining its true intent and meaning,
as indeed in construing most of the provisions of the

Constitution and its contemporaneous amendments, reference to the history and to the common law of England is generally the safest guide as to what was understood and intended at the time. In that history will be found the true sources of our institutions, for these are essentially and predominantly English. The legal and political institutions of England were constantly in the minds of the framers and of the people. The common law had long been regarded with affection and reverence as the birthright of Americans and the guardian at once of their private rights and their public liberties. Indeed, the Continental Congress, assembled in October, 1774, had declared the colonies entitled as of right to the common law.

The theory of the immunity of a state or of the United States from suit by an individual without its consent is frequently asserted to be analogous to the monarchical principle as to the immunity of the king from suit without his consent commonly expressed in the maxim that "the king can do no wrong." The idea seems to have been that in England it would be considered an invasion of the sovereignty of the crown and derogatory to its dignity to subject the king to a suit by an individual except with his consent, to be granted or refused in his arbitrary discretion. It is very doubtful whether any such idea finds support in the common law or history of England, or in the traditional usage and experience of that country to any such extent as is often insisted upon.

On the contrary, it had long been regarded in England as settled law that the subject was entitled to an effective legal remedy for any invasion of his legal rights by the king or the government. He had a right to sue the king for the restitution of property or money or for the recovery of damages for breach of contract, and to sue officers of the crown for any tortious acts. The practice established for centuries had been to present to the king a petition praying leave to sue him, and the custom had been for the king as of course to endorse on the petition his fiat that right be done. Thereafter the action proceeded as any other action between subject and subject. This right was conceded to aliens as well as to subjects. Although the leave to sue was nominally or theoretically granted as a matter of grace and not upon compulsion, it was in fact the constitutional duty of the king to grant it, and it was seldom denied. Under the common law, the subject was entitled as a matter of right — as one of the immemorial liberties of Englishmen — to inform his king of the nature of any grievance, and thereupon, in the language of Blackstone, "as the law presumes that to know of any injury and to redress it are inseparable in the royal breast, it then issues, as of course, in the king's own name, his orders to his judges to do justice to the party aggrieved."

The nature of the proceeding under a petition of right has been passed upon by the Supreme Court of the United States in several cases, and its decisions clearly show that the remedy is not to be regarded

as a mere matter of grace, but as a right to sue
and obtain redress in the class of cases to which it
applies. Thus, Chief Justice Marshall, delivering
the opinion of the court in Marbury *vs.* Madison
at the February term, 1803, said: "In Great
Britain the king himself is sued in the respectful
form of a petition, and he never fails to comply
with the judgment of his court."[1] In United
States *vs.* O'Keefe the court at the December
term, 1870, examined the nature of the remedy
in construing the act of Congress of July 27, 1868,
now section 1068 of the United States Revised
Statutes. Mr. Justice Davis, speaking for the
court, said: "This valuable privilege, secured to
the subject in the time of Edward the First, is now
crystallized in the common law of England. As
the prayer of the petition is grantable *ex debito
justitiae*, it is called a petition of right, and is a
judicial proceeding, to be tried like suits between
subject and subject. . . . It is of no consequence
that, theoretically speaking, the permission of the
crown is necessary to the filing of the petition,
because it is the duty of the king to grant it, and the
the right of the subject to demand it. And we find
that it is never refused, except in very extraordinary
cases, and this proves nothing against the existence
of the right. . . . If the mode of proceeding to
enforce it be formal and ceremonious, it is nevertheless a practical and efficient remedy for the
invasion by the sovereign power of individual

[1] 1 Cranch's Reports, p. 163.

rights."[1] And in the later case of Carlisle *vs.* United
States the court held that, under the proceeding
known as the petition of right, the government of
Great Britain accorded "the right to prosecute
claims against such government in its courts" not
only to subjects but to aliens.[2] Later still in the
famous case of United States *vs.* Lee, which was an
action at law to recover the property known as the
Arlington National Cemetery from the possession of
officers of the United States government, Mr. Justice
Miller, delivering the opinion of the court, said: "It
is believed that the petition of right, as it has been
practised and observed in the administration of
justice in England, has been as efficient in securing
the rights of suitors against the crown in all cases
appropriate to judicial proceedings, as that which
the law affords to the subjects of the king in legal
controversies among themselves."[3]

The remedy under the petition of right has continued unimpaired to the present time. The procedure is now regulated by the statute 23 and 24
Victoria, ch. 34, passed July 3, 1860. The statute
provides that the king by means of this proceeding
may be sued at law or in equity as the particular
case may require, and that the remedy afforded
"shall comprehend every species of relief claimed or
prayed for in any such petition of right, whether a
restitution of any incorporeal right, or a return of
lands or chattels, or a payment of money or damages,

---

[1] 11 Wallace's Reports, p. 183.
[2] 16 Wallace's Reports, p. 156.   [3] 106 United States Reports, p. 205.

or otherwise." In granting or refusing the petition, the king acts under the advice of the home secretary, and the latter is responsible to parliament in case he shall arbitrarily or wrongfully advise a refusal.

The petition of right, however, is available only in cases in which it is sought to obtain restitution of lands or goods, or, if restitution cannot be given, compensation in money, or where the claim arises out of a contract, as for goods supplied to the crown or to the public service. It does not extend to cases of tort. If the king personally should commit or threaten to commit a tort, such, for example, as a trespass, he could not be proceeded against in either a civil or a criminal court; the ordinary law courts have no means of restraining or punishing him personally or affording redress against him for any wrong done by him personally. Not only does the maxim that "the king can do no wrong" prevent any ordinary court from granting relief against the king himself, but the courts have no jurisdiction against him in cases of tort.

Nevertheless, this ancient and fundamental maxim never meant that the king was above the law or could violate the law with impunity, nor was it ever understood in any such sense as that everything done by the king was to be regarded as just and lawful. On the contrary, it was fearlessly proclaimed in the days of Bracton that the king was below the law and bound to obey it, and in his coronation oath he swears to observe and respect it.

But whatever might have been the personal immunity of the king, it had been settled at common law long prior to the adoption of the Constitution of the United States that immunity from suit did not extend to any officer or servant of the crown. The very exemption of the king from responsibility before the courts in cases of tort conclusively established the personal responsibility of some officer or servant of the crown, and the direction or authority of the king did not constitute any warrant or defense for a wrongful and illegal act done by any officer or servant. As the Supreme Court said in the case of Langford vs. United States: "The English maxim does not declare that the government, or those who administer it, can do no wrong; for it is a part of the principle itself that wrong may be done by the governing power, for which the ministry, for the time being, is held responsible."[1]

The boast of Englishmen for centuries had been that no officer of the government was above the ordinary law. In his interesting lectures at Oxford as a successor of Blackstone in the Vinerian professorship, Professor Dicey says: "In England the idea of legal equality, or of the universal subjection of all classes, to one law administered by the ordinary courts, has been pushed to its utmost limit. With us every official, from the prime minister down to a constable or a collector of taxes, is under the same responsibility for every act done without legal justification as any other citizen. The reports abound with cases in which officials have been brought before the courts, and made, in their personal capacity, liable

[1] 101 United States Reports, p. 343.

to punishment, or to the payment of damages, for acts done in their official character but in excess of their lawful authority. A colonial governor, a secretary of state, a military officer, and all subordinates, though carrying out the commands of their official superiors, are as responsible for any act which the law does not authorize as is any private and unofficial person."[1] And Anson in his "Law and Custom of the Constitution" points out that the English Constitution "has never recognized any distinction between those citizens who are and those who are not officers of the state in respect of the law which governs their conduct or the jurisdiction which deals with them." In the famous case of Entick *vs.* Carrington (1765), a secretary of state sought immunity as an officer of the crown from a suit for damages by pleading reasons of state for an unlawful act, but Lord Chief Justice Camden declared that "with respect to the argument of state necessity or a distinction that has been aimed at between state offences and others, the common law does not understand that kind of reasoning, nor do our books take notice of any such distinctions."[2] And one hundred years later, in the case of Feather *vs.* The Queen, Lord Chief Justice Cockburn declared that "no authority is needed to establish that a servant of the crown is responsible in law for a tortious act done to a fellow subject, though done by the authority of the crown, a position which appears to

[1] The Law of the Constitution, 8th ed., p. 189.
[2] Reported by Hargrave, 19 Howell's State Trials, pp. 1030, 1073.

us to rest on principles which are too well settled to admit of question, and which are alike essential to uphold the dignity of the crown on the one hand, and the rights and liberties of the subject on the other."[1]

Moreover, the rule of *respondeat superior* does not apply to the king. The conclusive legal presumption is that the king can do no legal wrong, and this leads to the further conclusive presumption that, in the eye of the law, he cannot authorize or direct a wrong. Every executive officer of the crown is, therefore, treated as if he were a principal, and as such is held personally responsible whenever any legal right of the subject has been invaded by him, although he may have acted under the direct order of the king, by his command and even in his presence. The civil irresponsibility of the king for tortious acts could not have been maintained with any show of justice if the officers and agents of the crown had not been held personally responsible for any illegal acts committed by them, and if the king had not been compelled to act through responsible agents. From the earliest times it has been deemed essential that the king should always act through an officer or servant, in order that there might be some one upon whom responsibility could be fastened. Lord Coke declares in his "Institutes" that "the king, being a body politique, cannot command but by matter of record." Custom and statute early required that all executive acts to which the sovereign was of necessity a party should be done in certain

[1] 6 Best and Smith's Queen's Bench Reports (1865), p. 297.

forms and authenticated by the signature or seal of some officer. The intervention of an officer was always necessary. In fact, some minister or officer of the crown can be held fully responsible for any illegal act. Anson states that "there is hardly anything which the sovereign can do without the intervention of written forms, and nothing for which a minister is not responsible."

Although the cases in England against officers of the crown were generally at law, there can be no reasonable doubt that the Court of Chancery, at the time when our Constitution was adopted, had full power, by means of the writ of injunction, to restrain an officer of the crown from violating the law where the remedy at law in a suit for damages or for possession of property, real or personal, would have been wholly inadequate and ineffective. The great state trial, known as the case of the Bankers,[1] in which Lord Somers was overruled by the House of Lords, left no doubt as to the principle and the jurisdiction of the courts in suits against crown officers. As Professor Goodnow has shown in his work on "Comparative Administrative Law," the English courts had long been accustomed in one way or another to control servants of the crown and executive officers of the government and to compel them to obey the law. All the great writs, which were at first prerogative writs, had been originally issued to control administrative or judicial officers. Such was the original function of man-

---

[1] Reported in 14 Howell's State Trials, pp. 1–114.

damus, habeas corpus, quo warranto, prohibition.
Injunctions, it is true, seem rarely to have been
made use of in England as a means of preventing
administrative action, and only a few cases can be
found where they were so used, but, on settled
principles, any administrative or executive officer
threatening to do an illegal act which would injure
the individual in his property rights was amenable
to the jurisdiction of courts of equity in controversies
requiring their intervention.

It is also true that no cases are to be found in
England where officers have been held responsible
in damages for enforcing an act of parliament or
have been restrained from carrying its provisions
into effect, but this, of course, is the result of the
legislative sovereignty of parliament and of the fact
that there are no constitutional limitations imposed
upon it. Nevertheless, the same principles which
make government officers in England subject to
the ordinary law and the ordinary courts for any
illegal act done or threatened would clearly authorize
the issuance of injunctions restraining the enforcement of an unconstitutional statute if there were any
constitutional limitations upon the legislative power
of the English parliament. Thus, for example, a
colonial statute, or a municipal or administrative
rule, by-law, or ordinance in conflict with an act of
parliament would be illegal and void, and, within
settled principles, its enforcement could be restrained if other grounds of equity jurisdiction
existed.

In the light of the long-settled and well-known rules of the common law, establishing the distinction between suits against the king under the petition of right and suits against officers of the crown for violating the legal rights of individuals, it is most significant and persuasive, if not convincing, that the framers of the eleventh amendment confined its language to suits directly against a state, and did not attempt to prohibit suits against officers of a state when acting as its representatives. They could hardly have intended that such a principle as that "the king can do no wrong" should have any place in our system of government to the prejudice of the constitutional rights of individuals. We have no king to whom it can be applied. They surely did not intend to afford less protection and less redress against the invasion of the rights of citizens by those in power than was afforded in monarchical England to the subjects of the king. They could not have been ignorant of the famous cases which had established the legal responsibility of all officers of the English government and their subordination to the jurisdiction of the ordinary courts of justice. They must have contemplated that state statutes might be passed in conflict with the Constitution of the United States, and that these statutes would necessarily have to be enforced or attempts made to enforce them by state officers. And they must have appreciated that if state officers, as agents of their respective states, were granted immunity from suit in a court of the United

States because they were acting for and on behalf of their states, the Constitution could in many respects be rendered wholly ineffective and nugatory.

The failure to prohibit suits against officers of a state must, therefore, have been intentional. Indeed, it is highly improbable that any one at the time conceived that the language adopted was broad enough to prohibit suits against officers of a state. On the contrary, it is proper to assume that the framers of the eleventh amendment did not intend to permit an officer of a state, while acting under the color or excuse of an unconstitutional state statute, to invade or deny any right guaranteed by the Constitution of the United States, or that such a state officer should be immune from suit in a court of the United States merely because he was acting in a representative capacity as an agent of the state. The courts of the United States were specially charged with the preservation of the Constitution, so far, indeed, as it can be preserved by judicial authority. The "Federalist" shows how clearly it was contemplated that the federal courts were to have power to overrule state statutes in manifest contravention of the Constitution. If state officers were withdrawn from the jurisdiction of the national courts, their oath to support the Constitution of the United States might become a mere empty ceremony of no enforceable obligation or sanction. If officers of a state could not be sued in equity in a federal court in an action to enjoin the enforcement of unconstitutional state statutes, many of the provisions of the Constitution, of equal authority with the eleventh amendment, might not be effectually enforceable except by the grace of the states. The prohibitions against the states, which existed when the eleventh amendment was adopted, such as that no state shall emit bills of credit, or make anything but gold and silver coin a tender in payment of debts, or pass any bill of attainder, or any ex post facto law, or any law impairing the obligation of contracts, or lay imposts or duties on imports or exports, might to a great extent be nullified and rendered practically ineffective, if officers of a state could not be sued in a federal court. Indeed, the thirteenth, fourteenth and fifteenth amendments would be deprived of a great part of their intended effect if state officers enforcing unconstitutional state laws and clothed with the power of the state could not be sued and enjoined in a federal court.

As each of these subsequent amendments, however, provides that "Congress shall have power to enforce this article by appropriate legislation," it has been suggested that this provision may be construed as limiting the prohibition of the eleventh amendment and as empowering Congress to confer on the courts of the United States jurisdiction of suits against states or state officers as an appropriate means of enforcing the later amendments.   Mr. Justice Shiras referred to this view in the case of Prout *vs*. Starr and said: "Much less can the eleventh amendment be successfully pleaded as an invincible barrier to judicial inquiry whether the salutary provisions of the fourteenth amendment have been disregarded by state enactments."[1]

The courts of the United States and of the several states have generally adopted and applied the English common law as to the amenability of executive and administrative officers to the jurisdiction of the ordinary courts and their personal responsibility for any illegal acts done by them or under their direction. There is no longer any question but that the eleventh amendment does not shield state officers from suits at law in a court of the United States to recover damages for any invasion of private rights under the color of an unconstitutional statute, or to recover possession of real property in the custody of such officers. The rule is axiomatic that no officer in this country is so high that he is above the Constitution of the United States, and that no officer of the law, state or national, may violate it under the color or excuse of a statute, national or state, in conflict with its provisions. The fact that an officer has acted on behalf of a state under the direction or authority of an unconstitutional statute, or under the orders of a superior, constitutes no defense to an action at law for restitution or for damages for any invasion of individual rights any more than the command of the king or the prime minister would constitute a defense in England. The alleged law is treated as a nullity and as absolutely void for all purposes, except perhaps as negativing the existence of malice or bad faith or

[1] 188 United States Reports, p. 543.

criminal intent. But it confers no warrant or authority and affords no defense or protection.

The fundamental reasoning upon which these conclusions are based is that the state, the abstract political entity, can speak and act only by valid laws, that an unconstitutional statute cannot be its legal act, that it cannot, legally speaking, authorize any act in conflict with the Constitution, that no officer of a state, not even the governor, can have any legal duty or legal executive function to disregard or violate the Constitution, and that whatever wrong is attempted in its name is to be conclusively imputed to its officer, who cannot plead his representative capacity. The distinction between the government of a state and the state itself is elucidated by Mr. Justice Matthews in the leading case of Poindexter *vs.* Greenhow.[1]

Most difficult, however, are questions which arise in connection with suits in equity to restrain state officers from enforcing state statutes alleged to be unconstitutional. The plainest principles of justice would seem in many cases to require a preventive remedy, for it might be of vital importance that an officer be restrained from doing an unlawful act to the irreparable injury of the individual. Manifestly, it would be unfair and unjust to tell the latter that he must wait until his rights have been violated or his property confiscated or destroyed. This point was first presented to the Supreme Court in 1824 in the leading case of Osborn *vs.* Bank of

[1] 114 United States Reports, p. 270.

the United States.[1] It was then declared, in
one of Chief Justice Marshall's famous opinions,
that, notwithstanding the eleventh amendment, a
circuit court of the United States had jurisdiction
in equity to restrain a state officer from executing
or enforcing an unconstitutional state statute when
to execute it would violate rights and privileges of
a complainant guaranteed by the Constitution of the
United States, and would work irreparable damage
and injury to him, for which no plain, adequate and
complete remedy could be had at law.

The general doctrine of the Osborn case has never
been departed from, and it has sustained innumerable
suits which have protected property rights from the
enforcement of state statutes in conflict with the
Constitution of the United States. It is no exaggeration to say that this doctrine, more than any
other, has rendered the Constitution an effective
shield against oppressive, tyrannical and confiscatory legislation, and compelled the states to obey
the supreme law of the Constitution. The reasoning
of Chief Justice Marshall is very logical and lucid,
and it is most convincing. If, as was then conceded
to be indisputable, the privilege or immunity of the
state as principal was not communicated to the
officer as agent, and if an action at law would lie
against the officer in which full compensation ought
to be made for a legal injury resulting from any
unlawful act done in pursuance of an unconstitutional and void statute, there existed no reason why

[1] 9 Wheaton's Reports, p. 738.

the preventive power of a court of equity should not equally apply to such an officer or why it should not restrain him from the commission of a wrong which it would punish him for committing. "If," continues the Chief Justice, "the party before the court would be responsible for the whole injury, why may he not be restrained from its commission, if no other party can be brought before the court?" It was pointed out that the very fact that the state could not be sued was a reason for permitting the suit to proceed in its absence against the officer or agent. We have here another example of how, in the evolution of legal principles, the same causes produce the same results. As in England the fact that the king could not be sued in the ordinary courts for a wrong led to the rule that his immunity or irresponsibility was not to be extended to his servants or agents and that the latter were to be held personally liable for whatever they did under the king's orders in violation of the legal rights of an individual, so with us the fact that a state could not be sued in a federal court led to the rule that its immunity or irresponsibility was not to be extended to its officers and that they were suable as responsible principals, even when acting under a state statute and as the agents or representatives of the state.

Chief Justice Marshall also said in the Osborn case that it might "be laid down as a rule which admits of no exception, that, in all cases where jurisdiction depends on the party, it is the party named in the record. Consequently the eleventh amendment, which restrains the jurisdiction granted by the Constitution over suits against states, is, of necessity, limited to those suits in which a state is a party on the record. The amendment has its full effect, if the Constitution be construed as it would have been construed had the jurisdiction of the court never been extended to suits brought against a state, by the citizens of another state, or by aliens. The state not being a party on the record, and the court having jurisdiction over those who are parties on the record, the true question is not one of jurisdiction, but whether, in the exercise of its jurisdiction, the court ought to make a decree against the defendants; whether they are to be considered as having a real interest, or as being only nominal parties," This reasoning was reaffirmed by the Supreme Court as late as 1872 in the case of Davis vs. Gray, [1] which was a suit against the governor of the state of Texas. But in later cases it has been repudiated, and the court has declared that "it must be regarded as a settled doctrine of this court, established by its recent decisions, 'that the question whether a suit is within the prohibition of the eleventh amendment is not always to be determined by reference to the nominal parties on the record.' " [2]

It may, nevertheless, be now interesting and valuable to re-examine the doctrine enunciated by Chief Justice Marshall and to inquire whether, after all,

[1] 16 Wallace's Reports, p. 220.
[2] In re Ayers, 123 United States Reports, p. 487.

it does not embody the true and sound rule which should govern this question, particularly in view of the fact that the decisions which have departed from his reasoning have failed to indicate any definite criterion to guide us in determining when a suit against a state officer is and when it is not to be deemed a suit against the state within the true meaning of the eleventh amendment. The question must be considered as if the jurisdiction of the federal courts had never been extended to suits by an individual against a state. The controlling inquiry in a suit against a state officer ought logically to be whether the relief or remedy sought can properly be granted in the absence of the state as a party defendant; in other words, whether the state is or is not a necessary and indispensable party; and this inquiry should be determined by the result or burden of the judgment which may be entered. If, for example, the suit is to enjoin the enforcement of an unconstitutional statute regulating rates or imposing taxes, it must be presumed that the state has not authorized the wrong, that it can have no legal concern or interest in a void enactment of its legislature, and that it cannot be heard to assert any right to have its officers violate the Constitution of the United States for its benefit. If, on the other hand, the relief or remedy sought will affect the property rights or funds of the state, or compel it to pay its debts, or require the specific performance of a contract by the state, or the doing or omitting to do any act by the state itself, the court must needs hold that it is a necessary and indispensable party, and that, as it cannot be sued in a federal court for want of jurisdiction over it, the suit must be dismissed. This dismissal, however, would not be for want of jurisdiction or judicial power over the individual state officer as defendant, nor because the suit was against the state — for the state was not a party and its presence was sought to be dispensed with — but because the state was an indispensable party defendant and the suit could not proceed in its absence. The result of recurring to this view would be to simplify the consideration of many cases and reconcile much conflicting reasoning. We should then have a definite and logical criterion to guide us in cases against state officers. If the court found that the state was not a necessary and indispensable party, the issue in such cases would be narrowed to the inquiry whether the relief should be granted against the officer within established principles of equity jurisprudence and procedure.

There remains the question as to enjoining criminal prosecutions. Should the jurisdiction of a court of equity be ousted simply because the state has authorized its officers to enforce unconstitutional regulations affecting property rights by a criminal instead of a civil action? The Supreme Court has held that, notwithstanding the general principle that a court of equity has no jurisdiction of a bill to stay criminal proceedings, it may nevertheless enjoin a state officer from instituting such proceedings where property rights are about to be invaded and destroyed through the instrumentality of an unconstitutional statute providing for its enforcement by criminal proceedings. The nature of an essentially civil question or controversy, such as one between shippers or passengers on the one side and a railroad company on the other as to the reasonableness of rates, cannot be changed by legislative fiat. The exercise of such a jurisdiction to restrain criminal proceedings has been found necessary in many recent cases where a defense on a criminal trial before a jury would afford no fair or adequate protection to those whose property rights were affected. The litigation, for example, under a bill in equity to restrain the enforcement of an unconstitutional criminal statute regulating rates presents a controversy of a civil nature with the officer and not with the state, and the only question is, whether a court of equity should intervene, or should leave those against whom criminal proceedings are threatened to their defense by demurrer to the indictment or trial on the merits. The latter will always be done when a defense at law will afford reasonably fair and adequate protection. But when a defense at law will not afford due protection and irreparable injury to property is threatened, there exists no reason why a court of equity should not intervene in such a case and grant protection and relief.

It may seem to many doubtful whether the two leading cases which are now attracting so much attention, namely, In re Ayers[1] and Fitts vs. McGhee,[2]

[1] 123 United States Reports, p. 443. [2] 172 United States Reports, p. 516.

necessarily presented any question under the eleventh amendment, and whether they should not have been disposed of solely upon the ground that a court of equity ought not to have enjoined the threatened suits or prosecutions. Probably neither of the suits in equity discussed in these two cases would have been maintainable under the general principles of equity jurisprudence even if the state had been suable in a court of the United States, for no irreparable injury was threatened and the opportunity of defense at law seemed to afford reasonable protection.

The question of the right to sue a state officer to restrain the enforcement of an unconstitutional statute regulating the rates and charges of railroad companies is now pending in some of its aspects before the Supreme Court in important cases involving statutes of Minnesota and North Carolina. These cases have been fully and ably argued and are under advisement, and they may lead to a reconsideration of some of the reasoning in the prior cases. A comprehensive decision may, therefore, shortly be delivered which will remove some of the reasons for the existing misunderstanding and conflict between the states and the federal courts.[1]

The time at our disposal renders it impossible to consider the many noteworthy and interesting cases which have arisen under the eleventh amendment and

[1] Ex parte Young (Attorney General of Minnesota), reported in 209 United States Reports, p. 123, and the case of Hunter (Sheriff of Buncombe County, N. C.) *vs.* Wood, 209 United States Reports, p. 205.

which frequently carry us into the realm of public law and statesmanship. The leading decisions are, of course, in the Supreme Court, but many instructive opinions will be found in the lower federal courts. The constant increase of governmental functions and of interference with individual liberty and action is certain to be a fruitful source of litigation in the future and will call for frequent consideration of the scope of the eleventh amendment.

In discussing the subject of suits to restrain the enforcement of state statutes alleged to be unconstitutional, we should not overlook or pass unnoticed the attempts made in recent enactments regulating rates and charges to coerce or intimidate railroad and other public service corporations into immediate obedience and abandonment of their constitutional right to appeal to the courts, by imposing upon them enormous and unreasonable fines and penalties, or by threatening them with the forfeiture of the protection of the government. Heavy fines or penalties are attached to violations of the law; and, as the transactions of these corporations are generally very numerous, disobedience of a statute, if only in good faith for the purpose of testing its validity, would in a few days involve the risk of bankruptcy. The avowed or ill-concealed purpose of these fines and penalties and of the resort to the criminal law is to prevent any interference by courts of equity. The idea, advanced in many quarters and under many disguises, seems to be that corporations shall be outlawed unless they consent to abandon their right to appeal to the courts for protection against unconstitutional statutes and void and oppressive enactments. This unfair spirit is widespread. For example, while the Federal Employers' Liability Act, recently declared unconstitutional by the Supreme Court of the United States, was under advisement by that court, President Roosevelt in his Jamestown speech criticized the railroad companies for having contested the validity of the statute and suggested that "the law should be such that it will be impossible for the railroads successfully to fight it without thereby forfeiting all right to the protection of the federal government under any circumstances."

The courts have repeatedly pointed out that the owners of property devoted to a public use are entitled to a fair and adequate judicial investigation if they contend that the rates or charges prescribed by a legislature are unreasonable and confiscatory. This is but recognizing that the owners of railroads and other property are entitled to a day in court, just as the humblest person is entitled to his day in court when his constitutional and vested property rights are invaded by the government. If the private property of the individual is to be taken for a public use, it would, of course, be obviously unfair and unjust to permit the legislature to say conclusively what should be paid to him, and deny him any adequate opportunity in the courts to review the legislative fiat. The same principle applies to public service corporations. They are entitled to appeal to the courts to pass upon the validity of any legislation which attempts to compel them to render services at a rate fixed by the legislature if they contend that such rate is unreasonably low and confiscatory; and, pending the judicial investigation, they ought not to incur the risk of accumulating and ruinous penalties. The New York Public Service Commissions Act of last year recognizes this in principle. But, instead of granting a fair hearing or providing for any judicial proceeding in which the reasonableness of the statutory rates may be promptly investigated, the constant effort seems to be to render resort to the courts so dangerous that property owners will abandon their right to a day in court rather than take the risks involved in allowing penalties to accrue and accumulate, which might subject their property to confiscation. Thus, in the recent New York gas statute, declared unconstitutional by the United States circuit court, no judicial investigation was afforded and the penalties imposed were at the rate of $1,000 for each overcharge or violation of the law. As the Consolidated Gas Company alone had upwards of 390,000 customers, an overcharge on only one month's bills, pending an attempt to test the law in good faith, would involve the fabulous total of $390,000,000 in penalties, or nearly five times the value of the whole property of the company. In fact, if the New York statute, at least in this respect, is not nullified by the Supreme Court on the pending appeal,[1] the Consolidated Gas Company may be

[1] Willcox *vs.* Consolidated Gas Co., 212 United States Reports, p. 19.

absolutely ruined for having asserted its legal right
to a fair judicial investigation before being compelled to accept what it insisted and what the court
has so far held was a confiscatory and unreasonable
rate; that is to say, for daring to insist upon a fair judicial hearing before being condemned.   The Kansas
statute regulating stockyards, which was declared
unconstitutional by the Supreme Court,[1] imposed
penalties which might have aggregated $15,000,000
in one day, or nearly twice the value of all the
property of the stockyards company.   The recent
railroad statute in North Carolina imposes fines
which would amount to $2,500,000 per day, and in
a few days would bankrupt the railroad companies.
The Minnesota railroad statute imposes penalties
which in one month might aggregate several hundred
million dollars.

Speaking of these penalties, United States Circuit
Judge Lochren justly said: " There is no question
but that such legislation is vicious, almost a disgrace
to the civilization of the age, and a reproach upon
the intelligence and sense of justice of any legislature which could enact provisions of that kind."

If any such policy of coercion and intimidation
can possibly be enforced by the state or national
governments, in any form or under any subterfuge
whatever, we shall no longer be living under a
constitutional government with effective guaranties
of individual rights and liberties.   If Congress or a

[1] Cotting vs. Kansas City Stock Yards Co., 183 United States Reports, p. 79.

state legislature can compel any class of persons to submit to an unconstitutional statute by imposing ruinous fines and penalties, or other provisions intended to operate *in terrorem*, or by threatening to deprive that class of the protection of the government, then the constitutional limitations imposed by the people can be readily circumvented and nullified, and our supposed rights and liberties will exist only in the grace or self-restraint of legislatures. One class is selected to-day, but another class will be selected to-morrow, depending only on the interest or prejudice or temptation or caprice of the temporary majority. Such an exercise of arbitrary and irresponsible power is in utter conflict with the whole theory of our institutions and in utter disregard and defiance of those fundamental and immutable principles of justice under which alone free governments can exist. As Chief Justice Marshall said in the great case of Marbury *vs.* Madison — and the court was then facing a hostile executive, a hostile Congress and a hostile public opinion — "The very essence of civil liberty certainly consists in the right of every individual to claim the protection of the laws whenever he receives an injury. One of the first duties of government is to afford that protection. . . . The government of the United States has been emphatically termed a government of laws and not of men. It will certainly cease to deserve this high appellation if the laws furnish no remedy for the violation of a vested legal right."[1]

[1] 1 Cranch's Reports, p. 163.

Some of the bills now pending before Congress propose to deprive the federal courts of the power to issue preliminary injunctions in these cases. This would be a policy fraught with immeasurable danger to property interests as well as to personal liberty. It would frequently amount to a complete denial of justice. The delay of litigation might readily be attended by ruin. But, undoubtedly, some reform is called for. There can be no question that preliminary injunctions against the enforcement of state statutes regulating public service corporations should never be granted without prior notice to the representatives of the people, and full opportunity for them to be heard, and then only upon the clearest showing of threatened irreparable injury pending the delay of a full hearing on the merits. Such cases ought not only to be given the earliest possible hearing, but the courts should insist that both sides proceed with the utmost expedition in the taking of testimony. A hearing in open court and not before a master would greatly facilitate this result. The people are entitled to a speedy determination of the questions involved in order that they may promptly have the benefit of the statute if it be constitutional, or that they may at once amend it if it be unconstitutional. There is no reason why in the majority of cases such a suit should not be ready for final hearing and actually be heard within sixty days, or why it should not be finally disposed of in the appellate courts within less than a year. It should have preference on all calendars. The Expedition Act of Congress, applicable to cases arising under the Anti-Trust and Interstate Commerce laws, would furnish a good model for cases involving the validity of state laws.

The conditions which now confront the people in many states, where statutes regulating public service corporations are often tied up for years by litigation, tend to create discontent, impatience and dissatisfaction with the courts and to engender a desire for revolutionary change from an intolerable situation. Laws regulating public utilities are often essential for protection against those who otherwise would have the power to make a prey of the necessities of the people, and it is disgraceful that the enforcement of such laws can be delayed by litigation for years after their enactment. As the delays in our criminal procedure are crying for remedy, so the delays in this class of litigation are crying for immediate and effective relief. It is of paramount importance that the people should be convinced that they can obtain in the courts, and especially in the federal courts, a prompt determination of all litigation affecting the validity of legislation regulating public service corporations which they or their representatives have deemed necessary for their protection against extortion or oppression. In most cases, however, it will be found that the representatives of the state are as much to blame for the delays as are their adversaries.

But, above all other considerations, stands the necessity for maintaining the absolute confidence of the people at large in the wisdom and impartiality of the federal judges, who are so often called upon to determine the validity of state statutes alleged to conflict with the Constitution of the United States and in so doing to administer justice as between the state and the individual — as between the majority and the minority. It should be a matter of profound concern to us as lawyers to make all laymen appreciate that the exercise of this jurisdiction by the federal courts is necessary for the preservation and perpetuation of the Constitution, and that it is right and just that every citizen should have the privilege of appealing to the national courts for the protection of rights and liberties guaranteed to him by the national Constitution. Equally important is it that the people should appreciate that in entertaining suits to restrain the enforcement of state laws alleged to be unconstitutional, the federal judges are only performing their duty according to their oath of office, which in the noble language prescribed in 1789 pledges them "to administer justice without respect to persons," to "do equal right to the poor and to the rich," and to "faithfully and impartially discharge and perform" their duty "agreeably to the Constitution and laws of the United States." An examination of the cases in which injunctions have been granted against the enforcement of state laws must satisfy any candid mind that in the great majority of cases the power has been impartially exercised, with tact and wise discretion, and that such injunctions have been granted only when property rights seemed to be threatened with irreparable injury. It would be too much to expect infallibility in all these cases. But errors are corrected on appeal.

Assaults upon our judiciary and unwarranted and unjust criticism of our judges undermine the people's trust in the courts and threaten the whole structure of our civilization. The United States judges are justly sensitive to public opinion and distressed by unjust and ignorant criticism. They know how important it is that they should retain public confidence. They realize, as their opinions constantly show, that "next to doing right, the great object in the administration of public justice should be to give public satisfaction." But they cannot sacrifice truth to popularity, the Constitution to present expediency. Those who assail the federal judges should bear in mind that the founders in their wisdom constituted the judicial power our bulwark against unadvised, hasty and tyrannical action on the part of those in power and our shield against "those sudden and strong passions to which we are exposed," and which, if unchecked and unrestrained, may lead to ruin. However unpopular and disagreeable the task may be of setting aside an act of Congress or of a state legislature, however painful it must be to any just man to become the subject of calumny, a federal judge has no choice, no discretion, no will of his own, but must hear and decide according to his conscience every case submitted to him within the jurisdiction of his court as conferred and imposed by the Constitution and laws of the United States. Let us always bear in mind the lofty words of the great Chief Justice in the case of Aaron Burr, in the decision which excited so much public prejudice and clamor one hundred years ago, when, speaking of the duty of a judge, he said: "If he has no choice in the case; if there is no alternative presented to him but a dereliction of duty, or the opprobrium of those who are denominated the world, he merits the contempt as well as the indignation of his country who can hesitate which to embrace." [1]

[1] 4 Cranch's Reports, Appendix, pp. 507-508.

CRITICISM OF THE COURTS [1]

THE attacks upon our courts which are constantly being published in the press throughout the country disclose a feeling of hostility towards the present system of administering justice that is probably the most portentous sign of our times. That the lawlessly inclined, who are fortunately still in the minority, should be hostile to those who are charged with the duty of enforcing and compelling obedience to the laws of the state or nation is not at all surprising and is perhaps almost inevitable in populous communities. But it is indeed surprising, and a legitimate cause for profound anxiety and misgiving, that thousands of honest, industrious, moral and law-abiding citizens should believe that the laws are not being impartially or justly administered, and that this erroneous belief should be inculcated, not only by the press and unprincipled demagogues and politicians but by reputable leaders of American labor and American public opinion, and even by educators. This belief has become so widespread and so fixed in the minds of vast numbers of our people of all classes, educated and uneducated, that only

[1] Read as a supplement to the report of a committee appointed by the New York State Bar Association submitted at the thirty-sixth annual meeting of the Association held at Utica, January 24, 1913.

the most exhaustive consideration and discussion
of the subject would be now adequate. Numerous
letters received by the sub-committee of the New
York State Bar Association, some of which are
submitted with its report, show the intensity of
the hostility towards the courts and the extent to
which it is based upon ignorance, prejudice and
malice. The fact that the writers of most of these
letters are sincere need not be challenged, but, this
being conceded, many of the statements show an
utter failure to investigate the facts and an entire
indifference to the truth, and some are obviously
puerile, or inexcusably inaccurate and reckless. On
the other hand, the spirit shown in letters from
some of the labor leaders must inspire the hope of
their loyal assistance in an impartial and thorough
investigation.   A great amount of good might be
accomplished by cooperation with them.   Such a
letter, for example, as that recently received from
Mr. Hugh Frayne, the general organizer of the
American Federation of Labor, indicates that exchange of views might lead to desirable results.
However irksome and laborious the task may be,
it would be a great service to the country at large
if some joint committee appointed by the New
York State Bar Association and the other bar
associations of the state would undertake to investigate all cases affecting labor or social legislation
and publish a report showing the true facts and
the principles of law involved in each case. The
pity is that many of the critics of our courts are

lamentably ignorant of the subjects about which they write or declaim, and — unconsciously and unintentionally in some instances — misrepresent and distort the facts.

It will be practicable at the present time to review only a few of the points suggested by the investigations of your sub-committee.

The subject of just compensation to employees for injuries received in the course of their work is one of the most important and far-reaching of those discussed by our correspondents, and its increasing difficulties and complexities call for much more study than we have been able to give it. The revolution wrought by machinery, the inevitable dangers attending its use, the crowding of men, women and children into factories and workshops require modifications in the rules of law governing the duties and responsibilities of employers. The rules of the common law, which are now condemned by so many and sought to be cast aside, were originally dictated by the soundest considerations of public policy, of practical affairs and government, and of justice as between man and man. The duties of the master toward the servant, as regulated by these rules, were humane and commensurate with the needs of the times that evolved them, and the rules themselves are still proper and just in the great majority of cases. Under them, the master is required to exercise the same degree of care for his servant that he should for his own safety, and he is bound to furnish a reasonably safe place in which his servant is to work, supply reasonably safe implements and machinery, select fellow-servants reasonably competent and prudent, and, where the nature of the business requires an overseer or superintendent, appoint one who is reasonably competent and prudent. The application of these rules regulating the conduct and duties of the master, in conjunction with the rules regulating the conduct and duties of the servant — such as the assumption of the ordinary risks of the employment, the fellow-servant doctrine, and the rule as to contributory negligence — unavoidably creates extremely difficult and complex questions. These rules are still proper and just in their application to such cases as involve the domestic relation between the farmer and his farm hands, the small contractor and his workmen, the householder and his house servants, the butcher, painter, carpenter, or blacksmith and his workmen. In all these cases it is, it seems to us, as true on principle to-day as it was half a century ago that the master is not bound to take more care of his servant than he may be reasonably expected to take of himself, and that a servant has better opportunities than his master of watching and guarding against the conduct and preventing the negligence of his fellow-servant. It is as true now as it ever was that, so long as liability is based on the theory or principle of negligence, a servant ought, generally speaking, to be held to assume the ordinary and obvious risks of the employment upon which he enters and for which he presumably stipulates for adequate and satisfactory compensation. Likewise, in the majority of cases, it is as true to-day as it ever was that the servant who has been guilty of contributory negligence should not be allowed to charge his master with responsibility for the injury. The reasoning of the judges establishing and maintaining these doctrines at the common law has never been refuted. Nevertheless, they are mere rules of law, subject to change, not by the judiciary, but by the legislature; and, in the opinion of the writer, there is no provision in the state or national constitution which would prevent their abrogation if this were deemed necessary or desirable by a legislative body.

But modern industrialism, the development of machinery, the employment of large numbers of men and women in crowded factories, and work in connection with dangerous instrumentalities of manufacture and transportation, etc., have changed conditions, so that what is still true of the farm, the household, the small artisan, the carpenter, the painter, the butcher, the grocer, etc., is not true of the busy hives of manufacture, of transportation by steam or electricity, or of other hazardous industries. The increase in accidents, the apparent certainty that many casualties are inevitable, the recklessness engendered by the modern struggle for existence, the increasing difficulty in many employments of measuring degrees of fault, the pressing necessities and improvidence of the poor: these and other considerations well warrant the interposition of the legislature as the lawmaking power of the state, in order to make changes in the law — changes which the courts should not attempt to make, for their duty or function is not to legislate but to declare what the law has been or now is. Instead, then, of abusing the courts, how much wiser and more decorous would it be for labor organizations, labor leaders, or social reformers to petition the legislature to amend the law, and to abandon the attempt to intimidate and coerce the judiciary into making the desired change. One of our correspondents speaks of "the venomous fellow-servant doctrine." Yet the responsibility for the continuance of that doctrine, if it has become undesirable in any employment or in all employments, rests wholly with the legislature and not with the courts. We should be surprised if any lawyer or student professing the slightest knowledge of American constitutional law would seriously assert that the legislature could not change that doctrine without amending or tinkering our constitutions.

It is, however, fit and proper to add that many lawyers and laymen are convinced that to abolish the existing rules indiscriminately in every case where the relation of master and servant may exist would be a mistake from the standpoint of public policy and practical justice, and that such a radical measure would do more harm than good. Certainly that is the judgment of competent observers of the operation of the British statute. A change in the law which would be wise if confined to large factories and hazardous employments, to labor in connection with dangerous machinery, to service on railroads, in large electrical works, etc., etc., might be extremely unwise, unjust and oppressive if applied, for example, to the small farmer, the artisan, the mechanic, or the householder. A rule concededly wise and just in the one case might be the extreme of folly and oppression in the other. An accident on a farm caused by the negligence or drunkenness of a farm hand might, under some of the proposed reforms or innovations, bankrupt the most prudent farmer for causes quite beyond his control; and a similar disaster might easily overtake the small artisan, mechanic, or householder, and sweep away the savings of years. It is, of course, no answer to say that the farmer, the artisan, the householder employing men or women can insure. Why should this form of taxation be levied upon slender earnings, which are frequently insufficient to make both ends meet? Why should the farmer or artisan of limited means be compelled to pay tribute to private insurance companies so often engaged in combinations to extort the highest possible premiums?

Let every master be responsible for his own negligence, but let the line be drawn short of making every master — every employer of another — the insurer of the safety of his servant to the extent of rendering the master liable for injuries resulting from no fault of his own but from the carelessness and negligence of the servant himself or of a fellow-servant.

An interesting example of the operation of a statute in connection with established rules of law will be found in the case of Knisley *vs.* Pratt.[1] The legislature had prescribed certain devices for the protection of women and children, including a provision that cogs on machinery should be properly guarded. In enacting this provision, as the courts were bound to assume by the settled rules of construction, the legislature was fully aware of the existing law in the state of New York in regard to the assumption of obvious and ordinary risks of employment by men and women of full age and capacity. The plaintiff in the Knisley case was a woman of full age and capacity, and she was well aware of the danger she was running in approaching too near machinery in operation. Had the statute been competently drawn, it would have provided—*assuming, of course, the draftsman and the legislature so intended*—that the rule of assumption of risk should not apply to cases within its purview; in other words, it would have provided that the master should be liable for any injury to a servant arising from the master's neglect to furnish the protection required by the statute whether or not the servant knew of such neglect or contributed in any way to his own injury. No provision of state or federal constitution prevented the legislature from enacting that the employer should be absolutely liable for the consequence of his own deliberate neglect to obey a statutory provision intended to protect human life and particularly the lives of women and children.

[1] 148 New York Reports, p. 372.

There is not the remotest intimation by the court in the Knisley case that the legislature could not so alter the law. After the decision in that case had been announced, a change in the law could have been readily made within a week, for the legislature was then in session — February, 1896. Yet seventeen years have passed without such an enactment, and in the meantime the Court of Appeals has been assailed before the whole country for its lack of sympathy with the poor and helpless and with social progress as evidenced among other things by this decision!

It is true that the doctrine of the Knisley case has been recently overruled by the Court of Appeals in the case of Fitzwater *vs.* Warren.[1] But many lawyers believe that the court might better have left this change to the legislature, which could have made it seventeen years ago if it had so desired, and not have furnished additional ground for the criticism that our courts are resorting to judicial legislation. Despite the Fitzwater case, it would still be wise for the legislature, *if it deems that the rule of law should be as now announced,* to enact a properly drawn statute declaring that whenever a statutory provision requires a master to supply guards or other protection for his servants in hazardous employments or in connection with the use of dangerous machinery, his neglect to do so shall render him liable irrespective of the doctrines of assumption of risk, fellow-servant's fault, or contributory negligence.

[1] 206 New York Reports, p. 355.

The manner in which nominations have been made in recent years for judicial office and particularly for the Court of Appeals has also invited very serious criticism on the part of our correspondents.

As is well known, the bar of the state of New York, with almost entire unanimity, has been endeavoring for many years to separate nominations for judicial office from other nominations, and thereby to divorce the bench from politics. It was the bar that has urged and forced the renomination of judges for the Court of Appeals on a non-partisan basis. It was the bar that urged and forced the renomination and election of Judge Gray and Chief Judge Cullen and other members of our highest court. It is simply slanderous to charge that any of the present judges of that great court were nominated at the request or dictation of what our correspondents call "the interests." The contrary is the truth; and the whole history and conduct of the court refute an accusation which is as contemptible as it is unfounded.

The bar of the state was practically unanimous in urging the passage last year of the measure known as the Judicial Candidates Bill, which proposed that the names of judicial candidates should no longer be printed in the party column on the general and official ballot, but on a separate ballot, or in a separate column of the voting machines, without party designation in either case, to the end that candidates for judicial office might be voted for as individuals and not as members or candidates of any political party. There was then an excellent opportunity for the professed social reformers and labor leaders who are so vehemently assailing our judicial system to aid in a movement to eliminate from politics the election of judges. But it was not availed of. The bill was defeated. It had little support from the press and very little, if any, support from social reformers or the representatives of labor. It will undoubtedly be introduced again this year; it has been once more approved by the Association of the Bar of the City of New York, and it will probably be again approved by the state association and by the bar of the state at large. Let the labor organizations now assist and cooperate in procuring the enactment of this law, and help to secure the election of judges on their own merits and personal character apart from considerations of political service or the favor or support of political leaders or bosses, or of any particular class.

A few years ago in the city of New York an earnest attempt was made by the bar to secure the election of justices of the Supreme Court on a non-partisan and non-political basis. A committee of members of the bar nominated lawyers of the highest standing in their profession, of recognized ability and learning and of unimpeachable character. These nominees were defeated, and to that defeat the labor organizations greatly contributed. These organizations then gave no support whatever to the movement to secure a separation of the courts from politics, and they were quite indifferent to the nomination of men of the highest character and of the highest qualifications for judicial office.

The plain truth on this point may serve and be useful as an object lesson. The least competent and the least experienced of the justices of the Supreme Court in the county of New York and elsewhere throughout the state are generally those who have been nominated because they were endorsed by labor organizations or were supposed to be acceptable to them. Everywhere throughout the country it is said that whenever labor organizations dictate or control the nomination of judges, they select lawyers of inferior education and talents and not of superior character and independence. It is high time that this truth was well pondered by labor.

One of the real causes for the discontent with the administration of justice in our state courts, and particularly in the larger cities, is that judges are nominated and elected not because of their legal ability and personal character, but because of their party affiliations or their supposed friendship or sympathy for or inclination to favor one class as against another. If the personnel of our Court of Appeals and Appellate Divisions has thus far been kept uniformly high and pure, it is because of the constant efforts of the bar. If labor organizations and the people at large will now cooperate with the bar, who in this matter are the proper leaders of public opinion, there will be infinitely less occasion for complaints of delay or incompetency or partiality in the administration of justice. The multiplication of incompetent judges means the multiplication of the causes of delay, new trials, denial or miscarriage of justice, expense, discontent and suspicion. The cure for these evils is with the people themselves, and it will be brought about only when they shall insist upon the nomination and election of lawyers of learning, character and independence.

It must be plain to all who have studied the facts and reflected upon existing tendencies that during the past twenty years the amendments to the laws regulating nomination and election to public office have served to strengthen and perpetuate the control of political leaders and political machines. Many bills introduced and loudly acclaimed as reforms have in truth proved to be not reforms at all, but steps in the dark and backward.

Some of our correspondents blame the courts for the "law's delay," yet there is no defect in our system for which competent judges are less responsible. In most instances of delay in civil cases, the blame belongs to the lawyers. Nothing has done more to bring the administration of justice into disrepute than the practice of adjourning cases term after term and year after year on excuses which sometimes are not well founded. There need be no unreasonable delay even in the city of New York, and would not be, if lawyers were ready to try their cases when they are first reached on the calendars. The judges are constantly complaining of the dilatoriness of the bar. Another cause of delay is the practice of bringing suits and taking appeals for the purpose of coercing settlements. A higher sense of professional responsibility ought to be cultivated, and there should be some severe penalty or professional ostracism for lawyers who abuse the process of the courts of justice and disregard the ethics of their profession.

In like manner, in criminal cases the real cause of delay in nearly every case is the failure or inability of prosecuting officers to press their cases diligently; and the frequent change in the personnel of our officeholders is likewise a cause of much delay. Whenever one official succeeds another, the period during which the new incumbent is learning what occurred before he came into office and familiarizing himself with the pending cases is so much time lost. Greater permanency in the tenure of office of prosecuting officers would probably conduce to greater speed and greater efficiency in the enforcement of the law. Nor can it be doubted that many public officials and their assistants do not feel the same degree of responsibility for the prompt dispatch of public business that they would feel if representing private clients. The remarks of Mr. Justice Scott in the recent case of People *vs.* Turley are indeed timely, and should be commended to the attention of all prosecuting officers throughout the state. He used the following language: "There is much well-justified complaint at the present time of the slowness with which the criminal law is enforced, and especially of the great length of time which is frequently permitted to elapse between a conviction and the review of the conviction by the appellate courts. Among persons not conversant with the rules of criminal procedure, the courts are not unnaturally, but most unjustly, charged with a large share of responsibility for this condition. The blame rests elsewhere. The appellate courts are powerless to act until the appeal is brought before them by those charged with that duty. When the matter is brought up for a hearing, the delay is ended, and the appeal is invariably promptly decided. The present is a particularly flagrant case. The defendant was convicted in March, 1909, and was almost immediately released on bail pending an appeal, under a certificate of reasonable doubt. The record is not voluminous, and the questions of law involved are neither difficult nor intricate, and yet the defendant has been at large for three years and a half before the appeal is brought on for argument. Of course under such circumstances the defendant was quite satisfied and was in no haste to have his appeal argued. The duty to bring it on promptly rested, as it rests in every case, upon the district attorney, who had it in his power at any time to force a hearing of the appeal by moving to dismiss it. This court has never shown itself to be unwilling to support and cooperate with the district attorney in compelling appeals in criminal cases to be argued with all reasonable promptness. The remedy for unreasonable delays in the final disposition of criminal appeals lies in his hands."[1]

[1] 153 N. Y. Appellate Division Reports, p. 674.

A number of important murder cases will be readily recalled where years have elapsed between the conviction of the accused and the argument in the Court of Appeals. Not only does this unnecessary delay deprive the judgment of conviction of much of its effect as an example and deterrent precedent, but in cases of reversal and new trials evidence is sometimes lost, and the guilty thus escape. In the latest reported murder case from New York county, People *vs.* Lustig,[1] the defendant was convicted of murder in the first degree in June, 1910, but the appeal was not brought on for hearing in the Court of Appeals until June 14, 1912, when it was decided and reversed within two weeks after the argument, viz., on June 29, 1912. In the meantime, as we are informed, material witnesses had disappeared, and the defendant is now at large on his own recognizance, and probably will not be tried again!

Another case of apparently inexcusable delay is People *vs.* Koerner.[2] The crime of murder was committed in September, 1896. The defendant was indicted within a month thereafter, and was convicted of murder in the first degree on March 1, 1897. The appeal was argued in the Court of Appeals within four court months, on October 22, 1897, and the judgment was reversed on November 23, 1897. The case was then re-tried, and resulted in a judgment of guilty of murder in the second degree on

[1] 206 New York Reports, p. 162.
[2] 154 New York Reports, p. 355; 117 N. Y. Appellate Division Reports, p. 40; and 191 New York Reports, p. 528.

March 15, 1898. The records of the courts show that the appeal from this judgment was not brought on for argument in the Appellate Division until December 12, 1906, and then resulted in an affirmance by that court on January 11, 1907, and that the appeal was not argued in the Court of Appeals until February 19, 1908, when the judgment was affirmed without opinion in less than three weeks!

Yet for the delays in these and similar cases the courts are criticized and their administration of criminal justice intemperately assailed by the press and other critics, notwithstanding the diligence of the judges in disposing of appeals when duly presented for their consideration.

It may be true that the pressure of innumerable cases compels the district attorney in New York county to delay the argument of appeals; but the remedy is to provide him with additional competent assistants and certainly not to indulge in indiscriminate criticism or unfounded abuse of the courts, or to resort to panaceas of reform in criminal procedure, which too often only multiply technicalities, deprive the individual of necessary protection, and create more or less confusion.

I shall now ask attention to the subject of injunctions in connection with strikes. I shall not argue the proposition that strikers in industrial controversies, or labor and labor organizations should not be above the law, or a law unto themselves. I assume that this is still a self-evident proposition in this state and may still be taken for granted. History certainly teaches us that in a free country no class can safely be released from the duty of obeying the laws, and that if disobedience be permitted in favor of the laboring classes, the industrious, honest and law-abiding laborer will be the worst sufferer in the long run. Nor will time be taken to point out that no civilized community can long permit any class to maim, or murder, or destroy property, or violently prevent others from earning their living, in order to coerce compliance with the demands of that class.

There would, of course, never be occasion for the use of injunctions in labor disputes if there were no threats of violence and no danger of injury to persons or property. If the labor organizations of this country will now earnestly, effectively and sincerely cooperate with the bar in the endeavor to put an end to violence and riots, which are the unfortunate but apparently inevitable attendants of every protracted modern strike, there will no longer be any occasion for condemning the courts on account of the issuance of injunctions, for there will then be no necessity for injunctions.

One aspect of the injunction problem is emphasized in the correspondence now submitted, and should be dealt with here. It is the matter of giving notice to the defendants before an injunction order is granted. Recently, when the United States Supreme Court adopted its new rules, including one as to injunctions, Mr. Gompers and other labor leaders loudly proclaimed that they had secured a great victory. Thus,

Mr. Gompers is reported in the "Literary Digest" of November 16, 1912, as calling the new rule a reform and "a step in the right direction, and one of the things labor has long been fighting for." But, as every one familiar with the subject well knows, there is nothing in the new rules that materially changes the pre-existing practice in regard to injunctions. The authoritative treatises on federal equity procedure by Mr. Foster and Mr. Street conclusively show this. No case has been cited to us and we have found none where the defendants enjoined were not granted by the courts as much facility in moving to dissolve or modify injunction orders as is provided for in the new rule. The learned and impartial editor of the "New York Law Journal" well said in the issue of December 11, 1912: "The only portion of the new procedure which has attracted the attention of the daily press is the rule regarding preliminary injunctions. This, however, is no more than an adoption of good New York practice, and, indeed, of good equity practice everywhere, viz.: that no *ex parte* injunction shall go out except as a stay-order to show cause why a preliminary injunction should not issue."

The case most often cited by labor leaders is known as the Debs case growing out of the Pullman strike at Chicago in 1894. If any fair-minded critic of the courts will take the trouble to read the unanimous, patriotic and inspiring opinion of the Supreme Court of the United States in the Debs case,[1] or what

---

[1] 158 United States Reports, p. 564.

ex-President Cleveland wrote on the subject in his book on "Presidential Problems," published in 1904, he will at once realize that the issuance of the injunction order and the subsequent punishment of Debs and his associates for deliberately and defiantly disobeying it were both proper and necessary.

For nearly twenty years and since the Debs case in 1894–1895, the labor leaders, agitators and demagogues of the country have been assailing the courts and denouncing "government by injunction" on the pretense, among others, that the judges denied the defendants in that case any opportunity to be heard, when as a matter of fact, they had the fullest notice and opportunity to be heard, but deliberately elected to disobey and defy the court. Indeed, in no jurisdiction is it true that a defendant is denied the right to a hearing upon the matter of an injunction against him, and the sub-committee has been unable to learn of a single case in which a judge has refused to give the defendant a hearing either upon an application to grant or continue an injunction, or to set one aside. A permanent injunction order is never granted without notice to those affected and an opportunity to be heard; nor is even a temporary restraining order issued without notice of hearing unless the danger of irreparable injury from delay be very grave, and then the order is made returnable at the earliest practicable date, so as to afford the defendants an opportunity to be promptly heard. If a temporary restraining order should be granted improvidently on insufficient

papers and upon an *ex parte* application, it is well
known that the order may be and frequently is
vacated immediately on the *ex parte* application of
the defendants. Most lawyers are familiar with such
cases. The fact is that laboring men have always
been afforded a hearing and a day in court in connection with injunction orders, and that no man has
ever been punished for contempt by an American
court without due notice to him and full opportunity to present his excuse or defense. Indeed, were
any man punished without notice and opportunity
to be heard, the order for his punishment would be
without jurisdiction and utterly void.

I may add that the lawless and violent among
the members of labor organizations will not in the
end gain any real liberty or advantage for the laboring classes, even if they succeed in abolishing the
writ of injunction in labor disputes and with it the
power of the courts to punish disobedience as a
contempt of court. Destruction of property and
assaults upon peaceful workingmen cannot permanently be tolerated in any civilized community.
Sooner or later, the government must afford protection in one form or another; otherwise chaos,
anarchy and barbarism are inevitable. If injunctions cannot be issued to restrain the violent and
protect the property of the innocent and law-abiding
citizen, simply because he is an employer or property
owner, then resort will finally have to be had to the
club of the policeman or the bayonet of the militia-
man or regular. It is no use blinking this certainty.

That was plainly the alternative presented by the Pullman strike; and President Cleveland then wisely preferred the orderly and peaceful procedure of a court of justice to the police power of the army. Under military rule, the laboring man may receive no hearing at all, and martial law with its arbitrary practices and despotic power will have to be substituted for the regular procedure of impartial courts of justice acting upon full notice to all affected and affording full opportunity to be heard.

The New York Code of Civil Procedure in sections 602-630 has long protected the rights of a striker as adequately as any other system of procedure, state or federal, domestic or foreign, and even better than the recent rule of the United States Supreme Court, which some labor leaders are acclaiming as a boon. Lest we forget, it may be useful to recall the exact language of section 626, which has been the statutory law since 1895. It is as follows: "Where the injunction order was granted without notice, the party enjoined may apply, upon the papers upon which it was granted, for an order vacating or modifying the injunction order. Such an application may be made, without notice, to the judge or justice who granted the order, or who held the term of the court where it was granted; or to a term of the appellate division of the supreme court. It cannot be made without notice, to any other judge, justice or term, unless the applicant produces proof, by affidavit, that, by reason of the absence or other disability of the judge or justice who granted the order, the application cannot be made to him; and that the applicant will be exposed to great injury, by the delay required for an application upon notice. The affidavit must be filed with the clerk; and a copy thereof, and of the order vacating or modifying the injunction order, must be served upon the plaintiff's attorney, before that order takes effect."

As is well known to all lawyers, a restraining or injunction order is never granted by a state or federal court in New York without notice to the defendants except when proof is submitted to the judge by affidavit or verified complaint which shows that, unless the defendant be immediately enjoined, irreparable loss or damage will result to the applicant before the matter can be heard on notice. If the court has sworn proof thus submitted to it that the defendants are threatening immediate injury to person or destruction of property, it is the duty of the judge — and may it ever be the duty of every American judge — to issue an injunction without delay, for delay in such a case would in most instances work a complete denial of justice.

If our system of equal laws impartially administered is to endure, the courts must continue to shield and protect the individual by means of injunction orders, and they should not be deprived of the power of exercising one of the most beneficent remedies afforded by any system of laws and one indispensable to the due and satisfactory administration of distributive and equal justice.

Some typical examples of misrepresentation of our

courts by leaders of public opinion will be recalled
in connection with the Tenement House Tobacco
case, the Bakers case, the Ives case, and other cases
involving so-called social legislation.[1]

When Mr. Roosevelt's statements in regard to the
Tenement House case were recently challenged by
four lawyers, including Senator Root, Mr. Milburn
and Mr. Marshall, as being inaccurate and likely to
mislead the voters of the state, he made no cor-
rection whatever, but urged the people to accept
his statements and those of a settlement worker
instead of the record of the case before the Court
of Appeals. This incident will serve to show the
difficulty of combating such inaccurate statements,
which are given the utmost publicity by the press
throughout the country, whereas the refutation is
generally ignored. A report of Mr. Roosevelt's
public comments, when his attention was called to
his manifestly incorrect statement of the decision
in the Tenement House case, quotes him as saying:

"I am informed that these four gentlemen attacked
the statements as being contrary to both the facts
and the law. The first was the case of the tenement-
house cigar manufacturers. Now I will read to
you what is said by one of the women who knows
the conditions of tenement-house life as few other
women, and as hardly any man, knows them, by
Florence Kelly in a book called 'Some Ethical Gains
through Legislation,' and I cordially commend to
Mr. Root and his associates who signed his protest

[1] See discussion *supra*, pp. 48–70.

to study that book and to ponder what is meant by the word 'ethical' in connection with legislation. Of the Jacobs case, to which I referred, Mrs. Kelly says: 'To the decision of the Court of Appeals in the case In re Jacobs is directly due the continuance of the tenement manufacture and of the sweating system in the United States and its present prevalence in New York.' That is the statement of a woman who, as regards knowledge of tenement-house conditions, knows so much more than those four great corporation lawyers that her little finger is thicker than their loins when you come to study what they know and what she knows of the subject of which they have ignorantly presumed to speak."

And yet all that these lawyers did was to point out the inaccuracy of Mr. Roosevelt's statements as to what the courts had held, and to suggest that this inaccuracy would be demonstrated by reference to the records of the courts, which are open to all who care to take the trouble to ascertain the truth.

It should be recalled in connection with any fair and candid consideration of the Tenement House case that the constitutional convention of 1894 had ample opportunity to change the rule in that case if it had then been thought to interfere with the attainment of "social justice." Although the subject was called to the attention of the convention, it was deemed advisable to make no change. The rule is reasonable and well-settled in the interpretation of constitutions and it was well known to the distinguished members of that convention that "where a clause or provision in a constitution, which has received a settled judicial construction, is adopted in the same words by the framers of another constitution, it will be presumed that the construction thereof was likewise adopted."

Another judicial decision denounced by Mr. Roosevelt a few days before the last election is the Knisley case discussed above. Speaking of this case, he told his audience, and through the press told the whole country, that "the Court of Appeals threw out the case and declared the law unconstitutional on this ground: that the legislature could not interfere with the liberty of that girl in losing her arm. . . . The trouble was that they knew law but didn't know right, and still more, as I have stated, that they had arrogated to themselves the right that the people should have — the right to decide what the common sense and justice of the people demand." Yet there was not one word anywhere in the record or in the opinion of the Court of Appeals which suggested that the act was unconstitutional or that the legislature did not have full power to change the common law rule in such cases and make the employer liable to his injured workmen or workwomen if he failed to comply with a statute prescribing guards or other protection for employees. The most superficial investigation would have disclosed the fact that the Court of Appeals has never intimated in any case that such a statute would be unconstitutional, and that in the Knisley case it neither had before it nor decided any question concerning the constitutionality of an act of the legislature.

Shortly before the election, Mr. Roosevelt caused to be published in the "Saturday Evening Post" of Philadelphia, under the title of "The Deceitful Red Herring," the following statement: "Our platform demands an eight-hour law for women in industries. . . . But the Court of Appeals of New York has said that the ten millions of people of my state have not got that right if they wish to exercise it. In New York the people did not ask for an eight-hour day — asked for only a ten-hour day for women. Then the Court of Appeals said that under their interpretation of the Constitution the small sweat-shop keeper or the big factory owner may work haggard women twelve, fourteen or sixteen hours a day, if he chooses, and we cannot stop it."

As a matter of fact, however, as the slightest investigation would have disclosed, the New York Court of Appeals had never decided anything of the kind. Moreover, there was in our state when Mr. Roosevelt published this statement a statute limiting the hours of labor for women to nine hours per day and fifty-four hours per week,[1] and for thirteen years prior to the recent amendment there had been a statute limiting the hours of labor of women to ten hours per day and sixty hours per week. These statutes had been regularly enforced for years, and their constitutionality had never been even questioned, so far as I have been able to ascertain.

[1] See the New York Labor Law, sec. 77.

Immediately after the publication of this article in the " Saturday Evening Post," a communication was addressed to the publisher by a well-known and reputable member of the New York bar, Mr. Alfred E. Ommen, pointing out the misstatement in regard to the Court of Appeals and conclusively showing its error; but this important periodical, with perhaps the largest circulation of any American weekly, saw fit to leave uncorrected this untrue and grossly misleading statement, and it has not yet withdrawn it, and probably never will do so.

Such is the tenor of the criticisms of the courts to be found in public speeches and in all forms of publication. They find constant repetition in the press, and carry the authority of distinguished leaders of public opinion and of men who at the present time have the ear and the confidence of the people. The statements of such men are naturally accepted as accurate and true. Who would believe it possible that any such statements as the above could be made by an ex-President of the United States unless they were true? As the draft of this report is being revised, an advertisement proclaims a renewal by Mr. Roosevelt of his attack on the courts, and a new assailant and critic appears in the person of Mr. William Randolph Hearst, who seems desirous to emulate Mr. Roosevelt in his abuse of the courts. The press at large continues to give the fullest publicity to all attacks on the courts and little or no space to any refutation of them. The judges are being misrepresented and assailed on all sides. They cannot defend themselves. The bar at large so far has seemed indifferent; and in the great forum of public opinion judgment is going by default.

If these misleading criticisms are not refuted, and the courts are not defended, they may bend before the storm of undeserved censure and the clamor of the crowd. There is grave danger that the judges will be unconsciously intimidated and coerced by this abuse. Indeed, some recent decisions are ominous. Is it not then fit and proper that the members of our profession should charge themselves specially with the task of defending the courts and placing the facts before the people? The bar associations of the country will never be called upon to render a greater service to the profession and to the community at large than that of stemming this tide of misrepresentation and intemperate abuse, and of restoring confidence in the learning, impartiality and independence of our judges, in the justice of their decisions, and in the necessity of their enforcing constitutional restraints.

GRADUATED OR PROGRESSIVE TAXATION [1]

THE recent message of the President to the Congress has strikingly brought to the attention of the American public the subject of graduated or progressive taxation upon inheritances and incomes. Acting upon the suggestions contained in the message, bills providing for such taxes have already been introduced in the House of Representatives. Amendments to the Constitution have also been proposed, one of which is to authorize Congress to tax inheritances amounting to or exceeding $50,000 and to levy an income tax without apportionment. The pending bills provide that successions of $10,000 and under and incomes of $4,000 and under are to be wholly exempted from the proposed taxes. The proposed graduated scales are to run from three-quarters of one per cent. on inheritances or successions over $10,000 and not exceeding $25,000 up to twenty-five per cent. on inheritances or successions exceeding $30,000,000, and from two per cent. on incomes exceeding $4,000 per annum and not exceeding $8,000 up to six per cent. on all incomes over $64,000. It is also suggested that Congress by

[1] Address delivered before the National Civic Federation at its annual meeting held in New York, December 13, 1906.

means of such taxes should seek, not merely to raise revenue for the support of the national government, but also to solve social problems by breaking up fortunes assumed to be swollen to an unhealthy size and thus bring about a redistribution of wealth.

In considering these proposed measures, it should be borne in mind that, if they or any similar propositions become laws, the result will be — and such undoubtedly is the intention — to exempt the majority of property owners from this form of taxation and to cast the burden upon a very small minority. It should also be realized that this proposed progressive taxation, particularly as to inheritances, is conceded to be only a first step, and that increases in the scale of progression are contemplated and will certainly follow. Indeed, the President declares that "at first a permanent national inheritance tax . . . need not approximate, either in amount or in the extent of the increase by graduation, to what such a tax should ultimately be." As the states have full power to levy taxes on inheritances and at the present time are deriving probably as much as $10,000,000 per annum from this source, it must be manifest that, if the scale adopted by Congress be high, the resources of the states will be correspondingly curtailed. In case of conflict, national taxes would take precedence over state taxes. We should also bear in mind that the power to tax is the strongest of all governmental powers, that it involves the power to destroy, that it generally knows no limitation except the discretion and

moderation of the lawmakers, and that of all powers
it is the one most liable to abuse.

From the time of the Declaration of Independence
to the present hour, the distinctive feature of the
American system of government has been equality
before the law, not merely equality of rights but
equality of duties and equality of burdens.   Equality
has been demanded in all things including especially
taxation.   The few exceptions in taxation, particularly in times of war, do not affect the general rule
that has been followed.   The courts have declared
that according to American ideals "common justice
requires that taxation, as far as possible, should be
equal."   Experience has shown that the only ef-
fectual protection against injustice and discrimination in taxation lies in the observance of some rule
of equality and apportionment;   and, although it is
true that absolute equality is not always attainable,
nevertheless an approximation to equality should
be regarded as indispensable.   As Hamilton said,
"The genius of liberty reprobates everything arbitrary or discretionary in taxation."   And Judge
Cooley in his famous work on "Constitutional
Limitations" said: "It is of the very essence of
taxation that it be levied with equality and uniformity, and to this end, that there should be some
system of apportionment.   Where the burden is
common, there should be common contribution to
discharge it.   Taxation is the equivalent for the
protection which the government affords to the
persons and property of its citizens; and as all are

alike protected, so all alike should bear the burden, in proportion to the interests secured." [1]

In proportional or equal taxation, whereby every property owner contributes toward the expenses of the common government according to the amount of property he owns or inherits, or according to the income he enjoys, we find a perfectly safe and consistent rule and a definite and logical principle upon which to work.   Proportional taxation subjects to the burden of government fairly and equally all property owners without distinction and without discrimination.   Nothing is left to mere discretion or to the play of arbitrary and irresponsible power, and no class is likely to be unjustly singled out or discriminated against.   Where property is as generally distributed as it is in this country, a proportional tax ordinarily reaches in one form or another a majority of the constituents of those who vote the taxes, and the sense of responsibility to these constituents operates as a conservative force and as a check upon unfair and unjust taxes, as well as upon improvident and extravagant expenditures.   A proportional tax generally creates a large body of taxpaying voters whose property interests impel them to watch their representatives closely and to hold them to strict accountability.   We then have taxation in its practical operation going hand in hand with representative responsibility, which was the cardinal principle for which our War of Independence was fought.   A legislator who is conscious of the fact that a large, if

[1] Constitutional Limitations, 7th ed., p. 705.

not a controlling, number of his constituents will feel
the burden of any tax he votes, is necessarily more
careful, more prudent, more economical and more
inclined to be just than if no such sense of responsibility exists.

On the other hand, where the great majority of
voters are to be exempted from taxation, and where,
accordingly, they will feel that they have no personal interest in governmental expenditures, they will
be likely to take little or no pains to see that there
is a fair apportionment of taxes which others must
pay, or any economy in governmental expenditures
for which others must provide. Their sense of
justice and civic duty will become blunted. It will
follow that, if the lawmakers are at liberty to enact
laws which exempt the great majority of their constituents from taxation and cast the burden and expense
of government on the few rich, frequently less than
two or three per cent. of the voters in their respective districts, there will exist no practical restraint
upon expenditure, but, on the contrary, every temptation to extravagance, wastefulness and injustice.

A graduated or progressive tax is necessarily
arbitrary, for there is no definite rule or principle
to apply to the scale. The rate, reasonable at
first, may ultimately become confiscatory. There is
nothing to check or stop the ascending scale. One
act of injustice will lead to another. The appetite
will grow and produce fresh injustice. If a tax of
twenty-five per cent. on large fortunes now seems to
some but a moderate beginning, where will the tax

stop, and who is to determine what is or is not reasonable and beyond what point a legislative body shall not go? A few advocates of progressive taxation have already suggested fifty per cent. as a maximum applicable to the so-called surplus of large fortunes, but others more radical and less responsible may readily advocate a tax of one hundred per cent. upon the surplus they regard as superfluous or unhealthful. There is, indeed, no limit to the possible ascent in the scale of progression, and no power to prevent abuse and oppression on the part of temporary and irresponsible majorities. The rich would then be completely at the mercy of mere numbers.

During the French Revolution, the experiment was tried under the name of compulsory loans. These loans finally absorbed fifty per cent. of such incomes as the majority of the legislative assembly saw fit to consider as *abondants*, and one hundred per cent. of all incomes which they thought were *superflus*.

The late W. E. H. Lecky, one of the most eminent historians of our day, wrote as follows of progressive taxation in his work on "Democracy and Liberty": "When the principle of taxing all fortunes on the same rate of computation is abandoned, no definite rule or principle remains. At what point the higher scale is to begin, or to what degree it is to be raised, depends wholly on the policy of governments and the balance of parties. The ascending scale may at first be very moderate, but it may at any time, when fresh taxes are required, be made more severe, till it reaches or approaches the point of confiscation.

No fixed line or amount of graduation can be maintained upon principle, or with any chance of finality. The whole matter will depend upon the interests and wishes of the electors; upon party politicians seeking for a cry and competing for the votes of very poor and very ignorant men. Under such a system all large properties may easily be made unsafe, and an insecurity may arise which will be fatal to all great financial undertakings. The most serious restraint on parliamentary extravagance will, at the same time, be taken away, and majorities will be invested with the easiest and most powerful instrument of oppression. Highly graduated taxation realizes most completely the supreme danger of democracy, creating a state of things in which one class imposes on another burdens which it is not asked to share, and impels the state into vast schemes of extravagance, under the belief that the whole cost will be thrown upon others."

In McCulloch on "Taxation," for fifty years the standard treatise in England on the subject, the following language is used: "It is argued that, in order fairly to proportion the tax to the ability of the contributors, such a graduated scale of duty should be adopted as should press lightly on the smaller class of properties and incomes, and increase according as they become larger and more able to bear taxation. We take leave, however, to protest against this proposal, which is not more seductive than it is unjust and dangerous. . . . If it either pass entirely over some classes, or press on some less heavily than on others, it is unjustly imposed. Government, in such a case, has plainly stepped out of its proper province, and has assessed the tax, not for the legitimate purpose of appropriating a certain proportion of the revenues of its subjects to the public exigencies, but that it might at the same time regulate the incomes of the contributors; that is, that it might depress one class and elevate another. The toleration of such a principle would necessarily lead to every species of abuse."

The well-known French political economist and scientist Leroy-Beaulieu in his works, *Traité d'Economie Politique* and *Science des Finances*, discusses at length the whole subject of graduated or progressive taxation, and condemns it as vicious in theory and unwise and unjust in practice. Among other things he says: "Progressive taxation constitutes actual spoliation. It violates, besides, the rule, established by all civilization, that taxation ought to be imposed with the full consent of the taxpayer; for, it is quite clear, that in this case, it is the mass of the voters who relieve themselves of the heavy weight of the tax and cast it upon the few, and these few do not consent, even tacitly, to the excess with which the government wishes to burden them. When the rate of the tax is equal for all, we can consider that the vote for the tax by the legislature carries with it the implied acquiescence of all the assessable; otherwise not. . . . Every system of progressive taxation, however attenuated, is iniquitous and dangerous."

And the same conclusions have been reached by a number of other distinguished French scholars and statesmen, among whom may be cited Thiers, Beauregard and Stourm.

The right of the states to levy progressive and unequal taxes on inheritances and testamentary dispositions is frequently sought to be upheld upon the theory that the power of our legislatures over successions to the property of decedents is unlimited, that the right to succeed is a mere statutory privilege, and that our lawmakers may arbitrarily grant or withhold that privilege at their will and discretion. It is, however, far from established that any such arbitrary and unrestrained power is vested in our state legislatures as that of denying wholly the right of inheritance or of testamentary disposition, or of discriminating in the regulation or grant of the privilege. The power to regulate the exercise of any right does not necessarily imply the power to deny it altogether. All rights of property as well as of personal liberty are subject to reasonable regulation, but this does not involve the power absolutely or arbitrarily to destroy such rights. The right of inheritance by children was not originally the creation of statute law at all, although the contrary is often assumed. It was a customary right long before the Conquest and prior to any statute of which we have record. It is treated by legal historians as "our common law of inheritance." In the latest authoritative history of the English law, that by Pollock and Maitland, the authors say that "in calling to our aid a law of intestate succession, we are not invoking a modern force," and that "the time when no such law existed is in strictest sense a prehistoric time." We find that it was a right already established in every one of the thirteen original states at the time the national government was founded; that it has always existed in civilized countries, so far as we have any knowledge; that it was recognized in the Twelve Tables as a right among the Romans; that it was a right long before among the Egyptians, and that it pervades the Mosaic law. A distinguished writer declares it to be the general direction of Providence itself. And Chancellor Kent said that "nature and policy have equally concurred to introduce and maintain this primary rule of inheritance in the laws and usage of all civilized nations."

The power of testamentary disposition undoubtedly developed as a limitation upon the right of inheritance and in order to prevent escheat for want of heirs. But however originating or evidenced — whether in old customs or in the practice of *post-obit* gifts — the right has been recognized from time immemorial. As Blackstone said in his "Commentaries," "in England this power of bequeathing is coeval with the first rudiments of the law, for we have no traces or memorials of any time when it did not exist."

Whatever may be the general language to be found in some judicial decisions, and whatever may be the extreme power of our state legislatures in the abstract, it is hardly conceivable that any state would attempt to escheat or confiscate all the property of decedents to the exclusion of children and near relatives, or that it would wholly deny the right of testamentary disposition. At any rate, if escheat or confiscation were ever decreed, it would have to be by laws applying equally to all decedents, and not merely to a selected class. The guaranties of the fourteenth amendment would prevent any discrimination.

But, however unlimited the power of the states may be in this regard, there can certainly be no doubt that it was not the intention of the framers of the Constitution of the United States to delegate to Congress the power to regulate successions to the estates of decedents or the privilege of testamentary disposition or inheritance. No one has yet seriously claimed that any such authority is within the legitimate sphere of the national government as contemplated by its founders. The power of regulating successions to the property of decedents was reserved to the states, and the courts would undoubtedly hold that any direct attempt on the part of Congress to regulate successions as such, or the ownership or transfer of property, was in excess of its powers. In dealing with successions, therefore, Congress can only exercise the power of taxation.

Yet it is urged that, as Congress has the power to tax successions, it may under the guise of exercising that power regulate inheritances and thereby break up large fortunes and force a redistribution of wealth.

In other words, the argument is that Congress may, under the cover or pretense of a tax law, accomplish indirectly an object which, for want of power, it could not accomplish directly, although the accomplishment of this object would constitute a deliberate encroachment upon the reserved rights of the states.

There is great danger in this view, and it opens the door to abuse by Congress of the power of taxation. If a federal statute purports on its face to be a tax measure, and in fact to some extent operates to that end, the courts cannot ordinarily set it aside, even though the motive for its enactment be to accomplish an object not entrusted to the national government. The jurisdiction of the courts is limited. Legislation which seeks to effect illegitimate ends cannot always be nullified. The power of Congress to levy a graduated inheritance tax as a revenue measure would be practically unlimited unless, in the particular instance, the law were so extravagant, and its unconstitutional object so plain, as to establish beyond doubt an unauthorized purpose. It is not within the province of the judicial power to determine whether a given tax which raises revenue is reasonable or unreasonable, or to inquire into the motives of Congress in enacting the law. The courts might not, therefore, be able to set aside an inheritance tax law passed by Congress even if it absorbed fifty per cent. or more of successions, although it might be quite apparent that the real object of the law was to invade the province of the states and to regulate inheritances in clear violation of the spirit of the Constitution.

Nothing could be better calculated ultimately to undermine our whole system of constitutional government than the idea that the courts alone are the guardians of the Constitution and that Congress may rightfully enact any statute which the courts cannot properly nullify. The truth is that the duty of preserving and defending the Constitution in all its integrity is vested in Congress and the President far more than in the courts, and that if Congress and the President do not observe the restraints and limitations imposed by the Constitution, Congress may pass many statutes which are unconstitutional in substance but which the courts cannot set aside. It is often urged that all questions of constitutionality should be left to the courts and not be passed upon by Congress or the President. The true doctrine, however, is that Congress should not enact and the President should not approve any statute which they, as the agents and representatives of the people, are not satisfied seeks to accomplish a legitimate end within the scope of some power delegated to Congress and not reserved to the states or to the people. They should first determine, as their oath of office requires, whether, according to their best judgment, the act is or is not constitutional. It was the distinct intention of the framers of the Constitution, and they so provided in express words, that every member of Congress, every senator and every representative, should be bound by oath or affirmation to support the Con-

stitution, and that the President, especially, should
be charged with the duty of preserving, protecting
and defending it to the best of his ability. This
duty extends not only to the letter but to the spirit
of the Constitution. It will be a lamentable exhibi-
tion of a lack of what may well be termed constitutional morality if, in the debates on the pending
measures, we shall again hear the suggestion that
objects concededly outside the scope of any power
delegated to the national government may nevertheless be accomplished indirectly by means of a
federal inheritance tax, in violation of the reserved
rights of the state governments.

If, in framing an inheritance tax law, Congress
will bear in mind that the regulation of successions to the property of decedents is a matter
solely within the jurisdiction of the states and
ought not to be usurped by the federal government, the object of raising revenue alone may lead
to fair and reasonable taxes levied impartially upon
all who should be called upon to pay for the support and maintenance of the common government
whose protection they enjoy. It would then, perhaps, be better appreciated that the states have
important and extensive governmental functions to
perform; that they need inheritance taxes for the
support of their governments, schools, charities,
police and public improvements, and that any
heavy federal succession taxes would embarrass
and cripple them. It is, of course, one thing to
resort to a federal inheritance tax as a temporary

war measure, when patriotism inspires ready acquiescence and willing sacrifice, and quite a different thing to establish such a tax as a permanent method of raising national revenue in times of peace and prosperity when the effect may be to withdraw that source of revenue from the states.

The subject of federal income taxes remains to be considered. There is no doubt that any state may levy income taxes. Nor is there any doubt that, under the federal Constitution as it now stands, Congress may levy an income tax provided it be apportioned according to population as required in regard to all direct federal taxes. There is also no doubt that Congress, by means of an excise tax, may reach income derived from any business or profession, and that any such tax, being essentially an excise tax on business, need not be apportioned but need merely be uniform throughout the United States. For example, a tax on the earnings of railroads and manufacturing businesses could be levied without apportionment, and it would produce a large revenue. It would also have the advantage of tapping income at the source. A tax by Congress on lands and personal property as such would, no one disputes, be a direct tax and subject to the rule of apportionment, and a tax on the income of property is in substance and practical and legal effect the equivalent of a tax on the property itself.

As Chief Justice Fuller said in the Income Tax cases: "The acceptance of the rule of apportionment was one of the compromises which made .

the adoption of the Constitution possible, and secured the creation of that dual form of government, so elastic and so strong, which has thus far survived in unabated vigor. If, by calling a tax indirect when it is essentially direct, the rule of protection could be frittered away, one of the great landmarks defining the boundary between the nation and the states of which it is composed, would have disappeared, and with it one of the bulwarks of private rights and private property." [1]

Nor is the rule of apportionment in itself unfair, even under the conditions existing to-day. If a direct income tax were now levied and duly apportioned among the states according to population as required by the Constitution, the smaller states would pay comparatively little and the more populous and richer states would have to bear what would seem to be their full share of national taxation. New York would then have to pay approximately ten per cent. of such a tax, Pennsylvania eight per cent., Illinois six per cent., Ohio five per cent., whilst Nevada would pay only one-twentieth of one per cent. and Delaware one-quarter of one per cent., although these two states have a representation in the Senate equal to that of New York and Pennsylvania. Indeed, ten states would have to pay more than one-half of any direct tax, leaving the balance to be divided among the remaining thirty-six states according to their population.   On the other

[1] 157 United States Reports, p. 583.

hand, if a graduated income tax such as is now proposed were levied without regard to apportionment,
and all incomes of $4,000 and under were exempted,
the effect would be to cast more than ninety per
cent. of the entire tax upon the inhabitants of less
than one-third of the states.

Nearly twelve years have passed since the decision
of the Income Tax cases, and there has been ample
time to amend the Constitution if the people had so
desired. But, instead of submitting an amendment
such as was introduced in the House of Representatives last week, it is suggested by some that an
attempt should be made to disregard or circumvent
the Constitution as interpreted by the Supreme
Court and to speculate on the change of its personnel
and the chance of different views on the part of new
incumbents. Surely, the simpler and wiser course
would be to ascertain the wishes of the people in the
manner provided by the Constitution. Assuming,
as is so frequently asserted, that the people generally
want a federal income tax, ratification of an amendment can be readily secured. The Congress, by
a vote of two-thirds of both houses, can at once
propose the necessary amendment, which will become effective when ratified by three-fourths of
the states. The ratification can probably be secured
in less than six months if there really exists any
general sentiment in favor of such an amendment,
for more than three-fourths of the state legislatures meet this winter. If deemed necessary, conventions could be called to meet within a few

months. In any event, the delay ought not to exceed fourteen months.

No student of our institutions can doubt that amendments to the Constitution will soon be thought necessary, and that such amendments will be submitted to the people. Our political system has not ceased to grow. Conditions are constantly changing, and powers which were adequate for the government of a federation of agricultural states may become insufficient for the necessities of the national government of a highly commercial and manufacturing people, with world-wide interests. Mr. Root's eloquent speech last night before the Pennsylvania Society has shown us how inevitably and irresistibly we are tending toward centralization. But it is mischievous and dangerous for the people to be taught that there is great or insurmountable difficulty in securing amendments to the Constitution in order to supply its defects or to meet changed conditions and that they must therefore accomplish their wishes by indirect means or by perverting delegated powers. The future contentment of the American people requires that they shall feel that they may readily, and are at liberty to, amend their organic law according to their mature judgment whenever they deem it necessary to do so. All that can be asked is that they shall act deliberately in the manner provided by the Constitution and under circumstances calculated to afford time and opportunity for error to be exposed, for theorizing and clamor and prejudice to exhaust themselves and "for the sober second thought of every part of the country to be asserted." If, then, it be determined to give to the national government the power to levy income taxes without apportionment, or to control successions to the estates of decedents, or any other power, the will of the sovereign people will have to be obeyed. But let us hope that when amendments are adopted they will be conservative and wise, that the reserved powers of the states will not be heedlessly curtailed to the embarrassment of the states, and that it will be appreciated that local self-government is still essential to the perpetuation of our republican and federal institutions.

THE DUTY OF CITIZENSHIP[1]

AT the outset of our deliberations, Republican delegates, it may be interesting to recall the circumstances of two prior national campaigns in which political symptoms and dissensions were quite analogous to those existing to-day. When the Republican state convention met in 1880, and again in 1896, the outlook for the success of the Republican party had for a time been discouraging. In each of these campaigns there were many who feared that the party had been disrupted and that its usefulness might be coming to an end. In each campaign a wave of false doctrine, sentimentality and prejudice threatened to drown reason amid the prevailing excitement, clamor and declamation. But in each courage and soberness came before November, and the common sense, honesty, sanity and patriotism of the American people supported the sound principles and policies of national and constitutional government for which the Republican party stands.

During the first three months of the political campaign of 1880, it seemed as though the Democratic candidate would be elected. The nomination of General Hancock had been received with great

[1] Address as temporary chairman of the New York Republican State Convention, at Saratoga Springs, September 25, 1912.

demonstrations of enthusiasm. He was personally attractive and popular, and at the outset little attention was paid to the fact that the platform of his party was radical and had declared in favor of "a tariff for revenue only" with the consequent abandonment of the protective system. The Republicans were not united; in some states they were hopelessly divided. The defection was certain to be large. In many Republican states the Greenback party, with its financial and social heresies, had increased enormously in strength, and it had nominated a national ticket. Maine had been carried in September by a combination of Greenbackers and Democrats. In November the Republican party was to lose New Jersey, California and Nevada, and, for the first time since the Civil War, it would fail to receive any electoral votes from the states south of Mason and Dixon's line. Yet Garfield was elected by 214 electoral votes against 155 for Hancock. New York, which had gone Democratic in 1876 with a plurality of 32,700, went Republican in 1880 with a plurality of 21,000. Thus we see that, although there was then schism and dissension in the Republican ranks, and although the party lost Maine in September and New Jersey, California and Nevada in November, as well as every southern state, its candidates nevertheless were elected.

A consideration of the circumstances of the campaign of 1896 will prove even more instructive and encouraging. The Republican party was then divided and threatened with ruin by defections.

The leaders in the national convention at St. Louis had courageously refused to bend to the demands and threats of a numerous minority, who were urging a radical platform and a radical candidate. A large number of Republicans had bolted, and they were loudly proclaiming that they alone represented the true and overwhelming sentiment of the party. According to them all else was fraudulent, and all who did not agree with them were accused of having been corrupted by the moneyed interests. It was evident that this faction had set out to rule or ruin their party, and, having failed to coerce it, were determined to overthrow it. They organized a new party, which they called the National Silver party; they assembled in convention at St. Louis amid excitement and posing and virtuous homilies about reformation and social uplift quite similar to those which we have heard during the past summer; they prophesied the death of the Republican party for its alleged betrayal of the people, and they proceeded to endorse the candidacy and views of Mr. Bryan. The Populist party, likewise largely composed of dissatisfied and discontented Republicans, held its national convention at St. Louis, went through similar political performances and emotional displays, and endorsed the Democratic candidate.

It would be difficult to exaggerate the enthusiasm in 1896 for Mr. Bryan. I comment upon it now in order that comparisons may be made and the lesson appreciated. Wherever he moved, immense and excited throngs pressed about him and wildly

cheered his utterances. Much of the character of
the present campaign was then in evidence. Bryan
preached a social reformation and a crusade against
established institutions, constitutional government
and the supremacy of the law. He played upon
envy, discontent and cupidity. He attracted to his
standard the remnants of Coxey's "army," which
two years before had marched to Washington, calling itself the "Army of the Commonweal of Christ."
In our country such movements frequently mask
in the robes of religion. Bryan denounced the
President then in office. He assailed our judicial
system, including the Supreme Court of the United
States. He posed as a knight-errant and crusader
who sought to uplift the poor and redress the wrongs
of the nation. He repeated all the exploded clap-
trap of demagogues. And his eloquence, together
with his apparent sincerity, made him a most dangerous candidate, far more dangerous than are our
opponents of to-day.

The combination of Democrats and former Republicans in 1896 was more formidable than if
their vote had been divided and the discontented
Republicans, Populists and Silverites had nominated
a separate ticket. It would have been easier to
defeat a divided enemy. Plurality and not majority
in each state determines the choice of presidential
electors, although a majority of the electors is
necessary to elect a President. The situation was
very critical because the times were hard, many
good reasons for discontent existed, thousands

of workmen in every state were unemployed, and agitators and demagogues found ready response to their appeals in the hearts of men who were suffering from hunger.

Yet, even under such conditions, the defense of constitutional government and established institutions was safe in the hands of the thoughtful, sober and patriotic people of the country. A complete revulsion of public feeling took place before November. The Democratic party, which four years before had carried the nation with a plurality of 381,000 and the state of New York with a plurality of 45,500, was defeated by the Republican candidate with a plurality of nearly 604,000 in the nation and over 268,000 in the state. McKinley received 271 electoral votes against 176 for Bryan. That great success was secured in the face of the fact that ten western states which are normally Republican went Democratic; in other words, the Republican candidates were triumphantly elected in 1896 although Colorado, Kansas, Idaho, Montana, Nebraska, Nevada, South Dakota, Utah, Washington and Wyoming all cast their electoral votes for Mr. Bryan.

The task of the Republican party in these prior campaigns was to bring home to the people the vital importance to them of the issues of those campaigns. Similarly our task in this campaign is to convince the voters of the country that they are again called upon to preserve the industrial system upon which the wages, income and property of millions

of American citizens are based, as well as to defend
the constitutional representative government under
which for more than a century we have maintained
political, religious and individual liberty and have
prospered beyond all nations.

At the beginning of this campaign and until
recently many Republicans were disheartened.
The menace to our institutions and future in the
possible success of the Progressive party and the
re-election of ex-President Roosevelt seemed as
portentous as was the menace of Bryanism in 1896,
in 1900 and in 1908. To some, therefore, it seemed
at first as if it might be their patriotic duty to vote
the Democratic ticket. Patriotism is ever more
than party. But these Republicans now realize
the folly of that course and the certainty that the
Republican party will maintain its solidarity. We
see clearly that the candidacy of Mr. Roosevelt is
doomed to defeat, and that only a desire to work
injury to the Republican party continues the campaign of the so-called Progressives.

I have examined the published record as to contested seats in the national convention of the
Republican party at Chicago, and I have endeav-
ored to ascertain all of the facts. I believe that
I have done so. In my judgment no fair-minded
person who will take the trouble to read the evidence,
who will look impartially at the facts and candidly
seek to discover the truth, can doubt the fairness
of the procedure or the correctness of the decisions.
Most of the contests were wholly unjustifiable, if

not fraudulent, and had to be abandoned. Indeed, it was shamelessly boasted by a well-known newspaper that the great majority of the contests had been gotten up in order to create a psychological effect, which, I take it, among plain people would mean the deliberate creation of a false impression. I will read you the language of one of the exemplars of the class of reformers who are too virtuous to remain in the Republican party and who profess to teach the people of this country political morality. The "Washington Times" contains the following in its issue of June 9, 1912: "For psychological effect as a move in practical politics it was necessary for the Roosevelt people to start contests on these early Taft selections in order that a tabulation of delegate strength could be put out that would show Roosevelt holding a good hand. In the game a table showing Taft 150, Roosevelt 19, contested 1, would not be very much calculated to inspire confidence, whereas, one showing Taft 23, Roosevelt 19, contested 127, looked very different. That is the whole story of the large number of southern contests that were started early in the game. It was never expected that they would be taken very seriously. They served a useful purpose, and now the national committee is deciding them in favor of Taft in most cases without real division."

Of the 238 contests finally filed on behalf of ex-President Roosevelt, 164 were abandoned. The contests which were not abandoned were decided on their merits. After studying the facts, I am con-

vinced that the Taft delegates were legally and
morally entitled to their seats.   Unfortunately, the
record is voluminous, and few will take the time or
trouble to read the evidence.   The cry of fraud is
misleading many.   But surely when such men as
Senator Root and the presidents of Columbia and
Cornell universities declare their conviction of
the integrity of the procedure and of the decisions, we may well rest satisfied.   In his speech
notifying President Taft of his renomination,
Senator Root said that neither in the facts nor
in the arguments produced before the national
committee, the committee on credentials, the convention itself, or otherwise, did there appear to
be any just ground for impeaching the honesty
and good faith of the decisions of the national committee.   He further declared to President Taft that
his title to the nomination was "as clear and unimpeachable as the title of any candidate of any party
since political conventions began."   Senator Root's
high character, his great services to the nation and
to the party, and his lofty sense of personal honor
and responsibility, entitle him to have his word and
his opinion under such circumstances unqualifiedly
accepted by the people of the state of New York.

The preference of the majority of the national
convention being clearly for President Taft, should
this majority nevertheless have cast him aside and
nominated Mr. Roosevelt because of threats of disruption of the party similar to those of 1896, or
because in a few states ex-President Roosevelt had

secured a larger primary vote than President Taft in hasty contests in which misrepresentation undoubtedly had led many astray? What course did patriotism dictate to the majority of the delegates? Ought they to have surrendered, and, because of clamor and threats of disruption of the party, put aside their own preferences and instructions for President Taft and nominated Mr. Roosevelt? There were reasons why this course would have been an act of folly as well as of injustice.

In the first place, the nomination of an ex-President of the United States for a third term would have been in violation of an unwritten rule established by Washington, Jefferson, Madison and Monroe, and followed ever since. The Republican party which, as a matter of sound principle and political ethics, had refused in 1880 to nominate ex-President Grant for a third term, notwithstanding his transcendent claims to the gratitude of the nation, could not stultify itself in 1912 by nominating ex-President Roosevelt for a third term.

The wisdom of maintaining this unwritten rule should be evident. The common sense of thoughtful, candid and patriotic men must convince them that nothing could be more dangerous than to permit any individual, however popular or eloquent, to wield the power of the presidential office for more than two terms. The New York convention of 1788, which ratified the Constitution of the United States, proposed an amendment to the effect "that no person shall be eligible to the office of President

of the United States a third time," and this undoubtedly has ever since been the sentiment of the
people of this state, although it was defied in 1880
when an attempt was made to force the nomination
of ex-President Grant for a third term, notwithstanding the fact that only five years before the
Republican state convention had declared in its
platform "our unalterable opposition to the election
of any president for a third term."

There is not time to discuss the genesis or wisdom
of this unwritten rule of political policy, which had
never been violated by any political party until the
nomination of ex-President Roosevelt by the Progressives. It is now pretended that there never
was any such rule or principle of political policy
and that Washington and Jefferson were governed
solely by considerations of their own personal convenience. Three quotations from Jefferson's writ-
ings ought to be sufficient to explode this pretense.
I take Jefferson because he is now one of the patron
saints of the Progressive as well as of the Democratic
party.

In January, 1805, shortly after his re-election,
Jefferson declared as follows: "General Washington
set the example of voluntary retirement after eight
years. I shall follow it. And a few more precedents will oppose the obstacle of habit to any one
after awhile who shall endeavor to extend his term.
Perhaps it may beget a disposition to establish it
by an amendment of the Constitution. I believe
I am doing right, therefore, in pursuing my prin-

ciple." Again in 1807 he wrote to the legislature
of Vermont: "I should unwillingly be the person
who, disregarding the sound precedent set by an
illustrious predecessor, should furnish the first
example of prolongation beyond the second term of
office." And fourteen years afterwards, in 1821, he
published his "Autobiography," in which he said:
"The example of four Presidents voluntarily retir-
ing at the end of their eighth year, and the progress
of public opinion that the principle is salutary,
have given it in practice the force of precedent and
usage; insomuch, that, should a President consent
to be a candidate for a third election, I trust he
would be rejected on this demonstration of ambi-
tious views."

But aside from all principle and precedent, the
promises deliberately made by ex-President Roosevelt to the people of the United States rendered his
candidacy impossible without what seems to many
a breach of faith. The facts speak for themselves.

On the 8th of November, 1904, President Roosevelt expressed to the people of the United States
gratitude for his election, and appealed to them for
their support and confidence during his second term,
undoubtedly having in mind President McKinley's example in 1901, when he had declared that
he would not accept a nomination for a third
term if it were tendered him, and had pointed out
that there were "questions of the greatest importance before the administration and the country,
and their just consideration should not be prejudiced

in the public mind by even the suspicion of the
thought of a third term." President Roosevelt's
language in 1904 was as follows: "On the 4th of
March next I shall have served three and one-half
years, and this three and one-half years constitutes
my first term. The wise custom which limits the
President to two terms regards the substance and
not the form. Under no circumstances will I be a
candidate for or accept another nomination." In
December, 1907, he reiterated this declaration, and
added the following words: "I have not changed
and shall not change the decision thus announced."
Yet on February 24, 1912, he gave to the press a
letter in which he said: "I will accept the nomination
for President if it is tendered to me, and I will adhere
to this decision until the convention has expressed
its preference."

The statesman who had thus pledged his word
could not break his promise to the people without
sacrificing the good opinion of many citizens. And
if the Republican national convention had joined
ex-President Roosevelt in a repudiation of these
solemn promises, it would have alienated a large
body of voters who still hold in reverence the
names and examples of Washington, Jefferson,
Madison and Monroe, and who still believe in
political consistency and morality, and it would
have put the party on the defensive throughout the
campaign upon an issue of plain and simple morals.
The Republican party, moreover, could not afford —
in fact it would have been hopeless — to ask for

the continued support of the country on any such terms.

Another reason why the majority in the Chicago convention should not have cast aside President Taft and nominated ex-President Roosevelt was because to have done so would have been an act of political treachery, ingratitude and dishonor. President Taft had earned and deserved renomination for great and faithful service to the nation and to the party. The custom generally followed had been to renominate a President who had served well and capably. The Republicans of New York had unanimously proclaimed in their platform of 1910, when ex-President Roosevelt himself controlled the state convention and dictated its policy: "We enthusiastically indorse the progressive and statesmanlike leadership of William Howard Taft, and declare our pride in the achievements of his first eighteen months as President of the United States. Each succeeding month since his inauguration has confirmed the nation in its high esteem of his greatness of character, intellectual ability, sturdy common sense, extraordinary patience and perseverance, broad and statesmanlike comprehension of public questions and unfaltering and unswerving adherence to duty." And nothing had occurred during the months intervening between this state convention and the national convention to shake that high and just estimate of the character and ability of President Taft. He had consented to run when he believed he could rely on the loyalty of

Mr. Roosevelt as his friend, and subsequent with-drawal would have been a personal humiliation.

In practical achievements, President Taft's ad-ministration had been notably successful and efficient, although not spectacular. It may be asserted with confidence that the laws enacted by Congress never had been administered more effectively, honestly and impartially than under President Taft. Without turmoil or agitation, and without threatening Con-gress, he had accomplished more in three and one-third years than his immediate predecessor in seven and one-half years. He had shown a consistent policy of real progressiveness and constructive states-manship. In every branch of government he had confirmed President Roosevelt's panegyric of 1908, when he urged the American people to elect Mr. Taft because of his pre-eminent qualifications for the office of President of the United States.

It may be true that after eighteen years of unselfish devotion and conspicuously efficient and faithful service to the American public, as solicitor general, United States circuit judge, governor of the Philippines, secretary of war and President of the United States, Mr. Taft had failed to secure popu-larity with the thoughtless, the discontented and the revolutionary, and with that part of the press that lives on sensationalism and muck-raking. But such popularity should hardly be the test of qualifica-tion for the great office of President of the United States. We know that Lincoln was so unpopular with the unthinking and impatient in 1864 that

he despaired of re-election and that he expected
defeat at the polls unless the army could save the
day and change public opinion by some striking
successes.

Popularity with the unreasoning and discontented
was easily within the reach of President Taft had
he sought it. In view of the prestige of his high
office and the reverence it commands, he had only
to practice the well-known arts of the demagogue
by which crowds are stirred and led astray — as
well known to him as to all who read history. He
had only to issue from time to time high-sounding
declarations about his staunch patriotism, his own
virtue, his uncompromising veracity, his self-sac-
rificing loyalty to duty, the infallibility of his judgment, the purity of his motives, and the corruption
and mendacity of his adversaries. He had only
to rail at corporations, at the builders of the industries of the country and at bankers and capital-
ists, in order to secure the applause of envy and
discontent. He had only to inveigh against predatory wealth to become at once the idol of predatory
poverty. But his self-respect would not allow him
to stoop so low and to pander to what is weakest,
if not basest, in human nature, and his sense of
duty would not permit him thus to degrade the great
office of President of the United States.

The ingratitude of republics is proverbial; yet
surely it would have been an unparalleled act of
ingratitude for President Taft's own party to refuse
him the renomination he had earned and deserved.

The lesson that the repudiation of President Taft by his own party would have taught the country and future generations would have been demoralizing. It would have constituted a warning to all our present and future public officers that with us Americans conspicuously efficient and faithful public service goes for naught, and that Republican public officers, from the President of the United States down to the lowest, must not expect to be judged by their acts, ability and character, but as they have succeeded in cultivating the applause of the unthinking.

The great issues before the people in the present critical campaign, however, are far more important than the personal qualifications, claims, or merits of the candidates. These issues are: (1) the constitutional right and power of Congress to protect American industries and to preserve our present industrial system; (2) the threatened overthrow of the representative system of government in state and nation by the introduction of the initiative, the referendum and the recall, and (3) the assault upon the administration of justice in American courts.

Upon the tariff question, there is an irreconcilable difference between the principles of the Republican party and those of the Democratic party. The one insists that it is the legitimate duty and function of Congress in levying taxes to protect American industries and wages, whilst the other insists that Congress has neither the right nor the power under the federal Constitution to do so. I shall assume that political platforms, although they may not be binding programmes, certainly are intended to embody a declaration of the political faith and principles in which the respective candidates believe and which they intend to represent. If this be not so, then why are platforms adopted?

The platform of the Republican party unqualifiedly pledges the party and its candidates to a protective tariff with duties so adjusted as adequately to protect American industries and wages. It concedes that readjustments must be made and that excessive rates should be reduced, but it insists that, in order to do so intelligently and fairly, correct information is indispensable. It favors securing this information by an expert commission and a non-partisan tariff board. It seeks the withdrawal of the tariff from politics in order that each industry may be dealt with on its merits by non-partisan commissions. It indicts the Democratic party for its refusal to provide funds for the continuance of such a tariff board and for the reckless and sectional tariff bills passed by the Democratic House of Representatives which wholly disregard the protection of American interests.

Senator Root declared at the national convention that the Democratic party did not want to ascertain the facts upon which a just protective measure could be framed, but intended that there should be no protection for American industries, and he further declared that the Democratic House of Representatives had framed and passed a series of tariff bills for revenue only with complete indifference to the absolute destruction that their enactment would bring upon great American industries. He asserted that "the American people have now to pass, not upon the abuses of the tariff, but on the fundamental question between the two systems of tariff-making."

This challenge the Democratic party met and answered in the first and cardinal plank adopted by its national convention at Baltimore, which pledged the party and its candidates to the ultimate attainment of the principles of free trade, because of the absence of power in the Congress of the United States to protect American labor and American industries. The plank reads as follows: "We declare it to be a fundamental principle of the Democratic party that the federal government, under the Constitution, has no right or power to impose or collect tariff duties except for the purpose of revenue." And there can be no doubt that this declaration was assumed not only to represent the present free-trade policy of the Democratic party but to be in full accord with Governor Wilson's personal views as an out-and-out free trader.

The people of the United States are, therefore, now asked by the Democratic party to vote in favor of the proposition that, no matter what foreign competition there may be, even from Asiatics, the American national government has neither the *right* nor the *power* to protect a single industry or a single workman. Such a proposition may well amaze and delight foreign countries, and no wonder they all desire the success of the Democratic party. Every other national government not only has the power to protect its industries, but has again and again exercised that power whenever the interests of its people demanded protection. The power in one form or another is being exercised to-day against American products by almost every government in the world, including the colonies of England, as witness Canada. The power would be exercised by England again to-morrow if it should appear to be for her interest to do so. Yet, no matter that our factories may be closed and our wage-earners thrown out of work as in 1894, 1895 and 1896, no matter how easily Europe and Asia could make our country their dumping-ground and could make a prey of our necessities after closing our workshops and destroying our industries, no matter how beneficial to all classes it may be to have a diversity of industries — the Democratic party, nevertheless, proclaims that our national government is powerless, and that there is neither the *right* nor the *power* to enact a tariff except for revenue.

We Republicans firmly believe that if there be one feature or element of right and power within the spirit and scope of the Constitution of the United States, and clearly vested in Congress, it is the right and power to impose duties for the purpose of protecting American industries and American labor. The very first tariff act, approved July 4, 1789, one hundred and twenty-three years ago, declared that one of its purposes, one of its objects, one of its inducing motives, was "the encouragement and protection of manufactures." Washington approved and signed that bill. Presidents Washington, Jefferson, Madison and Monroe — all of them of the generation that framed the federal Constitution — recognized the existence of the power to protect and recommended the protection of American industries. But the American people are now asked in 1912 to vote for a party and a platform which repudiate both the *right* and the *power* of Congress to protect American workmen, farmers and manufacturers.

It is impossible in this outline of issues adequately to discuss the principles and policy of a protective tariff. The details of that important and vital subject must be taken up and analyzed at other times. Generalizations would be of little value. The facts are readily at hand, and they demonstrate that the material welfare of the country and of nearly every class and section has been promoted by the protective policy, and it will continue to be so promoted. Although we may now be willing to face free competition with Europeans, we cannot be blind to the menace and danger of free competition with Asiatics. Just across the Pacific ocean, with constantly cheapening freight and passenger rates, are populations of 50,000,000 in Japan, 450,000,000 in China, 300,000,000 in India — 800,000,000 — who will furnish efficient labor at wages ranging from 10 to 30 cents a day for twelve hours' work on the same kind of machines at which American men and women are now working. Shall we open the flood-gates? Shall we elect as President the historian who, but a few years ago in the quiet and impartial atmosphere of his study, declared to the world his sympathy for needy Asiatics and his opinion that "the Chinese were more to be desired, as workmen if not as citizens, than most of the coarse crew that came crowding in every year at the eastern ports"?

This generation has had one bitter experience of Democratic tariff legislation. In 1892, the Democratic party was, for the first time in thirty-two years, placed in control of both houses of Congress and the presidency. It came into office committed to free trade, as it would now again come into office pledged to free trade. It passed the Wilson bill in August, 1894, and thereby took its first step towards the abandonment of the policy of protection for American industries. There followed, principally as the direct result of this Democratic tariff legislation and the antecedent menace, an acute period of industrial and financial depression. I had supposed that the fateful years 1894, 1895 and 1896 would never be forgotten by those who suffered through them. As Governor Wilson himself well said in his "History of the American People," in describing this period of misery: "Men of the poorer sort were idle everywhere, and filled with a sort of despair. All the large cities and manufacturing towns teemed with unemployed workingmen who were with the utmost difficulty kept from starvation by the systematic efforts of organized charity." This was also a time of unprecedented social unrest and discontent and of Coxey's ragged "Army of the Commonweal of Christ" crying for food and work. It was a period of misery and depression, of popular discontent and disturbance, of strikes, riots, destruction of property, murder and maiming in industrial disputes. No one could deny, as the historian pointed out, that the country had fallen upon evil times and that American workmen found it harder than ever to live.

We have only to recall to the people's minds the conditions of unemployment, poverty and misery which followed the last tariff legislation of the Democratic party, and compare conditions as they exist to-day. The people of this country will make a terrible mistake and a frightful blunder if they now vote to run the risk of a repetition of those days under the delusion that the currency system of the government was the cause of the business depression and misery that followed immediately upon the election of Cleveland in 1892 and the passage of the Wilson tariff law in 1894.

Many are now telling the people that the tariff is solely responsible for the high cost of living and for the prevalence of social unrest and discontent. Such phenomena are world-wide and exist abroad as much as, if not more than, they exist here. In England, which has no protective tariff, the complaint against the high cost of living has been even louder than here. The real causes of the

increase in the cost of living with us undoubtedly are: (1) enormous increase in the world's
supply of gold, necessarily diminishing the pur-
chasing value of the dollar, for the world's gold
production, which from 1850 to 1890 averaged
$120,000,000 per annum and was $130,650,000 in
1891, increased to fully $461,000,000 in 1911, (2)
rapid increase of population without a corresponding
increase of the production of food and other neces-
saries of life, (3) flocking to the city and abandoning
the farm, (4) appreciation in land values, (5) increase in the price of raw materials, (6) higher rates
of wages and decrease in the number of hours of work,
(7) better standards of living, (8) exhaustion of some
sources of supply, (9) extravagance in public expenditures, and (10) withdrawal of armies of civil servants
from productive industry. These are the principal and controlling causes that tend to the higher
cost of living; they are world-wide, and, if explained,
they will be easily understood and recognized by
intelligent and candid business men and workmen,
who will at once perceive that these causes will not
be removed in any degree by free-trade legislation.
Last year serious disturbances occurred in Europe
as a result of the prevailing high cost of food supplies
there, and the British board of trade is now making
an investigation into the cost of living, not only in
England but also in Germany, France and Belgium.
In fact, an international commission is at this moment inquiring into these causes. How preposterous it would be to say that the American protective

tariff was the cause of the high cost of living in free-trade England or elsewhere in Europe!

Nor is the protective tariff in any sense responsible for the spirit of social unrest and discontent except, perhaps, in so far as prosperity begets discontent and multiplies appetites. Throughout the civilized world in recent years there has developed a spirit of social unrest and discontent, of disregard of law, and of disrespect for moral principles and religious beliefs. To those who look below the surface, it is more and more evident that this world-wide symptom is due, in greatest measure, to the spread of Socialism. According to the teachings of the Socialists, avowed or unavowed (for many who are preaching its doctrines would resent being called Socialists), our entire social system and the system of laws under which we live are unjust and should be upset, property rights should be destroyed, and religious beliefs, which are the principal source of our respect for law and order and the rights of property, should be broken down. As an American student and writer has said, a single passage from Liebknecht stands fairly for opinions that may be quoted from twenty authoritative socialist sources in Europe. That passage is as follows: "It is our duty as Socialists to root out the faith in God with all our zeal, nor is any one worthy the name who does not consecrate himself to the spread of atheism." I believe that few American Socialists have gone to any such extreme, but such has certainly been the tendency and teaching of Socialism in Europe.

Unfortunately the atmosphere of the present campaign is calculated to obscure and hide the true issues in controversy and the real danger that lurks under so much noise, declamation and enthusiasm. An avowed assault and an open declaration of war on society, on our form of government, or on our courts of justice would bring the points so clearly before the American people that none of us could for a moment doubt the outcome. We Republicans would hail and welcome an open attack, because we know that the people would then quickly and overwhelmingly rally to the support of our party. The more openly constitutional government and our social system are attacked, the more strongly will they become cemented in the affection and reverence of the people.

Most of our political and social institutions which are now being assailed as antiquated are founded on truths which ought ever to be self-evident. These truths sound trite, but "trite truths are often the most valuable truths, though sometimes divested of force by their very triteness." We are constantly hearing talk about the principles of the Constitution being antiquated in the eyes of these modern iconoclasts, and the other day a leader of the Progressives in this state, who is himself a lawyer, referring to the Progressive judicial nominations boasted that they had selected men who did not believe in a "dead constitution." Yet these candidates are ready to accept a judicial office which they could not rightly fill for a minute without taking an oath to support the Constitution in which they do not believe.

When a truth, be it political, moral, or religious, is once discovered and established, it is eternal; it loses none of its vitality because it has grown old; it never dies. If some religious Progressive — and our political Progressives affect much of the religiously emotional — should now preach a new religion and proclaim that existing religions and their restraints should be cast aside simply because they are old, the dullest man would readily see the utter fallacy and wickedness of such an argument. Imagine any one seriously arguing that the Ten Commandments are worthless and dead as rules of human conduct and self-restraint because they are four thousand years old and were first enunciated in an age not so rapid as our own — in an age when there were no printing presses, no steam engines, no electricity and no talking machines! Yet, so long as our civilization endures, so long as human intelligence lasts, so long as religion shall continue to comfort and sustain and uplift men and women, so long will the Ten Commandments be sound and true rules of conduct and the fundamental basis of all religions. Likewise as to the great political documents evidencing the progress of the human race upward towards liberty, like Magna Carta, the Bill of Rights, the Declaration of Independence, the Constitution of the United States: they embody and declare principles of political justice and fundamental truths which are eternal; and whilst majorities at times may ignorantly and recklessly disregard them or cast them aside for temporary objects, they are as eternal and imperishable as are the Ten Commandments.

Of the many revolutionary schemes in the Progressive platform, both national and state, one of the most dangerous and far-reaching is the proposal to destroy the representative character of our government by substituting direct action by the people in place of action by legislatures and officers elected by the people. This is to be accomplished through the initiative and the referendum. The movement is doubly important at the present time because, as is well known, the Democratic candidate for the presidency, after teaching directly the contrary for many years, has become a recent convert to these ideas. Although such a scheme might be beneficial or harmless in the little town meetings of New England, in small municipalities, or in agricultural states having a homogeneous population less in number than some of the counties of the state of New York, the initiative and the referendum would be wholly unsuited to an empire such as ours with a population of nearly 100,000,000, or to a state such as New York with a population of nearly 10,000,000. Would it not be absurd and preposterous to have the thousands of bills annually introduced in Congress passed upon by the people at large, and would it not be equally absurd and preposterous for a state like New York, passing hundreds of bills every year, to give a small minority the right to compel the submission of every statute to the vote of the people? Would it not be little short of calamitous to have those least qualified to understand and appreciate the changes they were making pass upon and control legislation? The result would be chaos.

The great men who founded our system of constitutional government were thoroughly familiar with the theory and operation of pure democracy or direct action by the people, as distinguished from representative government. They saw the past failures of pure democracy and the danger of any such system, and they deliberately declined to adopt it. In speaking of "the equal rights of man," Jefferson declared that "modern times have the signal advantage, too, of having discovered the only device by which these rights can be secured, to wit, — government by the people, acting not in person, but by representatives chosen by themselves."

The plain truth is that the trouble with our legislatures and with Congress is the character of many of the men whom the people elect. The remedy is in the hands of the voters. If they will elect capable and honest men to legislative, executive and judicial office, we shall have a cure at once. We need a remedy, not a poison.

Those who urge the introduction of the initiative, the referendum and the recall base their argument on the ground that some of our legislators and elective officers are incompetent or dishonest, and that, therefore, the people should reserve the right to control their actions and remove them. But if our legislators or other elective officers are incompetent or dishonest — if they are not truly representative of the people who elect them — then obviously the fault lies with those who choose them, and the remedy is to take such measures as will ensure the election of competent, honest and representative men. If the people are now too busy to concern themselves with the selection of honest and capable representatives, is it reasonable to expect that they will concern themselves about the merits of hundreds of statutes which they do not half understand, or about the qualifications of the officers they have elected and would recall? The fault is not with our representative system of government, but either with the party organizations that often nominate incompetent or dishonest men, or with the voters who tolerate such nominations and elect such candidates. Our system of government, as every system of free government, is based on the assumption that the people will conscientiously exercise the elective franchise, and unless we can depend upon an honest, sober-minded and patriotic majority to exercise that franchise, our system of government must ultimately prove a complete failure. The conscientious exercise of the elective franchise is not merely a privilege — it is the highest duty of citizenship. With the great increase in population, political parties and party organizations undoubtedly have become a practical necessity, and leadership is equally necessary; but it has also become indispensable that these party organizations shall be conducted honestly so as to represent truly the wishes of their party constituents. The urgent duty of citizenship is to see to it that these party organizations are conducted honestly and in a representative manner; but this is not to be accomplished by disrupting or destroying the great parties. Instead of pulling down the temple, we should drive out the money-changers. Instead of killing we should cure. What we urgently need is legislation providing for fair and honest party primaries and facilitating independent candidacies, and then we should go farther and impose a penalty or tax upon all qualified citizens who fail to cast a ballot at the annual primaries and elections prescribed by law.

The initiative, the referendum and the recall would not cure present evils, but would in fact only intensify and perpetuate them. The power and control of unrepresentative and irresponsible party machines would be largely increased instead of being curtailed. Better men would not be nominated and elected, but quite the contrary; the self-seeker, advertiser and manipulator alone would be nominated. The exercise of the initiative, the referendum and the recall would be determined by exactly the same people who now control our nominations and elections. It is absurd to suppose that the very men who so often choose incapable or dishonest representatives or neglect to vote at all would exercise greater efficiency in supervising legislation, in recalling public officers and judges, or in setting aside judicial decisions.

Equally absurd is the idea of legislation by popular vote. The importance of framing laws and constitutional amendments in clear and exact language and the impracticability of doing so without careful consideration and discussion and comparison with existing provisions, as in legislative committees, must be recognized by all thinking men. Our system of laws is becoming more and more complex every year, and unavoidably so. The people at large cannot be expected to know and understand a great and extremely complex system of laws, and it is no reflection on them to say that they cannot grasp the details of legislation any more than it would be to say that there are few men in the community competent to administer as judges the unavoidably intricate system of laws under which we live.

We have only to look at recent experience in the state of New York in regard to the adoption of constitutional amendments, the most important function that can be exercised by a voter, to appreciate the folly of the proposed remedies. The total vote for and against these amendments has frequently been less than one-half — and at times barely one-quarter — of those who actually voted at general elections. Thus, to take three recent experiences: the total vote cast in 1909 on an important constitutional amendment was only 477,105 as against a total vote the year before of 1,638,350; the total vote in 1910 on another important constitutional amendment was 664,892 as against 1,445,249 votes for the gubernatorial candidates, and seven amendments submitted in 1911 were defeated with an average total vote of 621,678. Similar and even more striking experiences will be found in other states. Is it likely that there would be a fuller or more representative and intelligent expression of public understanding in regard to complex legislative enactments, or in regard to the recall of judges or other public officers, or of judicial decisions than we find now in the case of important constitutional amendments?

To render judges subject to recall would be utterly destructive of the character and independence of our judiciary. No self-respecting lawyer would serve on the bench under such conditions. An upright judge should fearlessly declare and enforce the law without regard to popular agitation or political pressure. Frequently he is called upon to decide between the individual on the one side and a clamorous majority on the other side of a case before him. Take, for example, our situation in New York with Tammany Hall controlling a majority of the voters of the city. The legislature at the dictation of Mr. Murphy passes another infamous Levy Election Law avowedly intended to prevent independent nominations even for the bench. The judges declare the act unconstitutional and protect the minority in their rights, just as we saw them protecting the Progressives a few weeks ago. According to Mr. Roosevelt and Mr. Straus, however, Tammany Hall should have the power to punish these judges by recalling them and should have the right to pass such disgraceful and tyrannical legislation by resort to the initiative and the referendum! Indeed, it is impossible to conceive of a scheme more surely calculated to shatter all our constitutional rights, as well as all certainty in the law. Chief Justice Marshall would have been repeatedly recalled for unpopular decisions which are now universally applauded even by the Progressives. Imagine the spectacle of recalling a Cullen or a Gray because he had dared to decide against the clamor or wishes of a majority controlled by Tammany Hall!

I have nowhere seen a stronger statement of the objections to the recall of judges than in John Stuart Mill's work on "Representative Government," published in 1861, where he said: "If a judge could be removed from office by a popular vote, whoever was desirous of supplanting him would make capital for that purpose out of all his judicial decisions; would carry all of them, as far as he found practicable, by irregular appeal before a public opinion wholly incompetent, for want of having heard the case, or from having heard it without either the precautions or the impartiality belonging to a judicial hearing; would play upon popular passion and prejudice where they existed, and take pains to arouse them where they did not. And in this, if the case were interesting, and he took sufficient trouble, he would infallibly be successful, unless the judge or his friends descended into the arena, and made equally powerful appeals on the other side. Judges would end by feeling that they risked their office upon every decision they gave in a case susceptible of general interest, and that it was less essential for them to consider what decision was just, than what would be most applauded by the public, or would least admit of insidious misrepresentation."

Probably no more crude, impracticable, or absurd scheme was ever proposed by any one claiming to have the first and elemental ideas of American constitutional government than the proposition to render subject to recall or reversal by a majority vote all decisions in constitutional cases affecting statutes passed under the police power. The term "police power" is the most comprehensive that could have been employed. Most of our individual rights are covered by that term; and when the Progressives say that a statute passed under the police power shall be valid and enforceable, notwithstanding the courts may declare it to be arbitrary, unjust and unequal and hence unconstitutional, if a temporary majority see fit to overrule the courts, they propose that practically all the most vital and cherished of our supposed inalienable individual rights — our personal and religious liberty — shall in final result be at the mercy of any temporary majority. In ultimate analysis, the proposition for the recall of judicial decisions would mean that the majority should act as umpire in any dispute as between themselves and the minority.

The hatred of the courts which the Progressives now share in common with the Socialists, Anarchists and Populists, and that part of organized labor and labor unions typified and represented by such men as the McNamaras, the Debses and the Parks (who in truth shamefully misrepresent the great majority of law-abiding and patriotic members of these organizations), has forced into this campaign an unparalleled attack upon our judicial system and the administration of justice.

When the New York state Progressive platform was first given to the press on September 3rd, the judiciary plank read as follows: "We heartily indorse the declarations of our national platform respecting the judiciary and favor their embodiment in the organic law of the state. We condemn the past attitude of the New York Court of Appeals toward various important and humane measures of social legislation."

The unprecedented indecency of this attack upon the Court of Appeals immediately produced such a storm of indignation throughout the state that the clause appears later to have been amended so as to eliminate that sentence. The final form given to the public omits this denunciation of the highest court of our state, and confines the plank to the proposals of the national platform. I have time now to discuss only two of these planks.

The Progressives declare in their extraordinary and revolutionary platform: "We believe that the issuance of injunctions in cases arising out of labor disputes should be prohibited, when such injunctions would not apply when no labor disputes existed."

This should be compared with substantially the same declaration in the Bryan platform of 1908, in which the Democratic party declared: "We deem . . . that injunctions should not be issued in any cases in which injunctions would not issue if no industrial dispute were involved."

It must seem incredible that the cultured and talented man who now stands on the Progressive platform soliciting the votes of the people was the President of the United States who in a formal message to Congress on January 31, 1908, on the subject of injunctions in labor disputes, used the following language: "Even though it were possible, I should consider it most unwise to abolish the use of the process of injunction. It is necessary in order that the courts may maintain their own dignity, and in order that they may in an effective manner check disorder and violence. The judge who uses it cautiously and conservatively, but who, when the need arises, uses it fearlessly, confers the greatest service upon our people, and his pre-eminent usefulness as a public servant should be heartily recognized."

During the campaign of 1908, President Roosevelt fiercely denounced Mr. Bryan and Mr. Gompers for the plank above quoted but which he has now adopted. He then wrote a long letter to Senator Knox in which he exposed the danger and dishonesty of this plank. It would be necessary to read the whole of the letter in order to appreciate President Roosevelt's indignation and horror that Bryan and

Gompers should favor such a proposition. I shall quote only a few sentences as samples of the whole. President Roosevelt then wrote as follows: "This is the plank that promises the 'remedy' against injunctions which Mr. Gompers asked of Mr. Bryan's party. In actual fact, it means absolutely nothing; no change of the law could be based on it; no man without inside knowledge could foretell what its meaning would turn out to be, for no man could foretell how any judge would decide in any given case, as the plank apparently leaves each judge free to say when he issues an injunction in a labor case whether or not it is a case in which an injunction would issue if labor were not involved." Later the President continued: "Mr. Gompers, now Mr. Bryan's open and avowed ally, has, in the letter here quoted, attacked the federal courts in unmeasured terms of reproach because, by a long line of decisions, the equity courts have refused to make an outlaw of the business man, because his right to carry on a lawful business under the peace of the law has been protected by the process of injunction, because in a word one of the most vital and most fundamental rights of the business world — the right of a business man to carry on his business — has been sustained and not denied by the processes of the courts of equity. This sweeping attack of Mr. Gompers upon the judiciary has been made in a frank and open effort to secure votes for Mr. Bryan." Mr. Roosevelt concluded the letter as follows: "But there is another account against

Messrs. Bryan and Gompers in this matter. Ephraim feedeth on wind. Their proposed remedy is an empty sham. They are seeking to delude their followers by the promise of a law which would damage their country solely because of the vicious moral purpose that would be shown by putting it upon the statute books, but which would be utterly worthless to accomplish its avowed purpose. I have not the slightest doubt that such a law as that proposed by Mr. Bryan would, if enacted by Congress, be declared unconstitutional by a unanimous Supreme Court, unless, indeed, Mr. Bryan were able to pack this court with men appointed for the special purpose of declaring such a law constitutional."

The Progressive plank against the power of the courts to punish for contempt is equally revolutionary. It declares in favor of depriving the courts of the power to punish for contempt except after a trial by jury.

The crusade to deprive the courts of the power to punish for contempt began at the time of the Chicago strike of 1894 when Eugene Debs and his fellow-conspirators were found to be guilty of open, continued and defiant disobedience of an injunction order of the United States court which had been duly served upon them. It will be recalled by most of you that if the courts had not then had power to punish for contempt without a prior conviction by a jury — and imagine the chance of an impartial jury-trial during the continuance of a great riot —

the Debs party would have had the city of Chicago and the great railway commerce passing through it completely at its mercy.   All who want to know the facts and to realize the danger from the condition of affairs then existing should read Mr. Cleveland's account of the strike in his book on "Presidential Problems," published in 1904, and the opinion of the Supreme Court of the United States unanimously upholding the punishment of Debs and his associates for contempt.

The power of the courts to punish for contempt has, from the earliest history of jurisprudence and as far back as the annals of our law extend, "been regarded as a necessary incident and attribute of a court, without which it could no more exist than without a judge," and "a court without the power effectually to protect itself against the assaults of the lawless or to enforce its orders, judgments, or decrees against the recusant parties before it, would be a disgrace to the legislature, and a stigma upon the age which invented it." The Supreme Court of the United States declared in the Debs case that "this is no technical rule. In order that a court may compel obedience to its orders it must have the right to inquire whether there has been any disobedience thereof. To submit the question of disobedience to another tribunal, be it a jury or another court, would operate to deprive the proceeding of half its efficiency." [1]

[1] 158 United States Reports, p. 594–595.

The bait now offered to the lawless and mis-
guided among the laborers of America by Mr.
Roosevelt is the abolition of the only effective
means of preventing violence and the destruction
of property in labor disputes, first, by taking
away from the courts the power to issue injunctions and, secondly, by emasculating the power
to enforce obedience to their orders and judgments. Of course, if any such revolutionary and
anarchistic measures were now embodied in the
organic law of this state, as proposed by the
Progressive state platform, the community would
be placed completely at the mercy of the violent
and the lawless. Is it not lamentable and humiliat-
ing to see an ex-President of the United States and
an ex-member of his cabinet and ex-ambassador
thus pandering to the mob spirit for votes?

In conclusion, I want to add that the American
people know where President Taft and Vice-President
Sherman stand on every great question before the
people. They have been tried and not found want-
ing. These candidates can be trusted and relied
upon to keep every pledge of their party's platform.
If anybody can now tell where Governor Wilson
stands, except as a free trader, a radical and an
opportunist, he is much more discerning than most
of us are. The glory of our party is that for fifty-six
years, in victory and in defeat, it and its candidates
have stood consistently and uncompromisingly for
the principles of human liberty and human progress.
It is still the party of principle and of progress, as

it is the party of protection for American labor and industry. President Taft would be entitled to the gratitude of the whole nation, irrespective of party, if the only service of his administration had been his attempt in good faith to withdraw the tariff from party politics, to introduce some system in fixing the amount of necessary protection to be determined by experts and non-partisan boards, and to establish business-like methods of economy and efficiency in every department. Great honor, too, will the future historian record to his credit when recounting that in a period of political upheaval, of social unrest and discontent, of impatience with law, of pandering to revolutionary instincts, he stood as President of the United States firmly, uncompromisingly and sturdily for the right, and put all his trust and confidence in the sober second thought and profound patriotism of the American people, in their attachment to law and orderly progress, and in their determination that the American system of constitutional representative government "shall not perish from the earth."

NOMINATING CONVENTIONS [1]

THE Direct Primary Law of 1911 [2] abolished all political conventions except the state convention, but the Direct Primary Law of 1913 [3] went further and abolished the state convention, striking the article on conventions and even the definition of a convention from the text of the law. Although the new law contains in section 45 a provision that nothing therein contained shall prevent a party from holding a party convention, to be constituted in such manner and with such powers in relation to formulating party platforms and policies and the transaction of business relating to party affairs, as the rules and regulations of the party may provide, not inconsistent with the Election Law, it was clearly the intention of its framers that such party conventions should not deal with the most important subject which parties had theretofore dealt with, namely, the nomination of candidates for public office. Indeed, section 46, as amended in 1913, expressly provides that designations of candidates for party nominations shall be "by petition only" in the manner provided in the Election Law.

[1] Remarks before the Committee on Suffrage of the Constitutional Convention of the state of New York at Albany, June 16, 1915.

[2] Laws of 1911, ch. 891. [3] Laws of 1913, ch. 820.

The privilege of nominating elective state officers by means of delegate conventions thus denied by the Election Law of the state of New York ought, in my judgment, to be recognized as essentially a constitutional right, which the legislature should not be at liberty to abridge. The right to assemble peaceably for the purpose of nominating candidates is certainly a political right of permanent importance and vital concern to all citizens, and it should be guaranteed by constitutional provision and not left to abridgment or denial by the legislature. The present state constitution regulates the qualifications of voters, the registration of citizens entitled to vote, and the creation of registration and election boards. But it does not contain a single provision in regard to nominations for office, even for the office of governor, although nominations for state offices are of far greater importance to the body politic than many of the matters now regulated by constitutional provision or recited in the bill of rights. I desire to urge upon your careful consideration the value of nominating conventions as a constitutional right.

The constantly increasing functions of the modern state have made the executive and administrative departments the most important and powerful branches of government, and the increasing complexity of governmental machinery has rendered it absolutely essential that competent and trained public officials should be chosen. Government has become an extremely difficult and scientific business, and special capacity, training and expert knowledge are more and more required in executive and administrative office. The test of a good government is more than ever its ability to produce good administration. If we are to have efficient and avoid wasteful administration, the greatest care must be exercised in selecting candidates. As Governor Throop said nearly a century ago, "there is perhaps no part of the duties of citizenship which requires more sound judgment and honesty and singleness of purpose than those relating to the nomination and election of executive and administrative officers." Indeed, good government depends in final results much more on the ability and character of the men who administer it than upon laws or institutions. The maxim, constantly on the lips of so many, that a government of laws and not of men is the controlling desideratum, may be grossly misleading, for the best system of laws in the hands of incompetent, inefficient and dishonest administrators will produce far worse results than an inferior system in the hands of competent, efficient and honest public officials. The most difficult task and the highest duty that our electorate are ever called upon to perform is, therefore, the selection of candidates for elective state office. In order to perform that duty, it is imperative that there should be adequate and reliable means of information, full opportunity for conference, exchange of views, debate and criticism as to the capacity and character of candidates, and effective methods of cooperation and organization in support of qualified candidates.

The selection of a governor for the great state of New York, containing more than 10,250,000 inhabitants and comprising a political constituency larger than any other in this country, is certainly a matter of vital and profound concern to the whole body politic, to every citizen, to every community, to every party, to every class, to every interest. If the short ballot be now adopted, the successful administration of the whole state government will practically be staked upon the selection of qualified candidates for governor. All hope of governmental reform, efficiency and economy will then necessarily depend upon the statesmanship and character of one man, who will be vested with full executive and administrative powers over a population and a territory larger than some of the nations of the world. A wise and safe choice will be infinitely more essential and more difficult than in the past. In fact, if the views of certain advocates of the short ballot prevail, we are to vest all this power in the governor for a term of four years, without restraint of any kind except his sense of responsibility to the people, and without any effective check upon his will or caprice. We should have to trust him absolutely. We should, in truth, have precisely the definition of an elective despotism and tyranny — beneficent if we are so fortunate and blessed as to secure an exceptionally able and high-minded statesman for governor, baneful if an incompetent, untrained, or scheming politician or demagogue should be elected. The governor would then have it

immediately within his power to become an absolute
state boss through the use of an enormous and
constantly increasing patronage, directly or indirectly
reaching and touching every election district in the
state. He would be able to break party lines
asunder, to promote the interests of any group or
faction, to punish adversaries, to cater to any
class, to sacrifice the rights of minorities, to sub-
stitute his will or caprice for the policy of his
party, to permit waste and extravagance, to dictate
who should be his successor. A competent candidate for governor who would be so well known and
tested as to be safely relied upon to resist this
temptation would indeed be a phenomenon. If
history teaches us that there is anything certain in
human nature, if experience, which is of far more
value than any mere reasoning or theorizing, has
again and again demonstrated any practical and
eternal truth in politics, it is that unrestrained
power inevitably leads sooner or later to abuse and
tyranny, and that no one official, be he emperor,
king, president, or governor, can safely be entrusted
with any such power.

We should bear in mind that the extreme advocates of the short ballot, by eliminating all require-
ments for the approval and consent of the senate
in regard to the appointment of heads of the great
state departments, would make the governor supreme and independent of the legislature, even more
independent and powerful than is the President under the Constitution of the United States. I sincerely

hope that the Convention will not make this grave mistake. The number of state elective officers should not be reduced to less than four, namèly, governor, lieutenant-governor, comptroller and attorney-general. The comptroller should be made an auditing officer charged with supervision as such over the various departments of the state and independent of the appointing power. The attorney-general should be made the head of a department of justice and the responsible legal adviser of the governor and of every state official. And the heads of all the great departments should be appointed by the governor, with the approval and consent of the senate. No governor should be given the unrestrained power to appoint or to remove the heads of all departments. The requirement of the consent of the senate is a necessary and salutary restraint upon all governors, good or bad. It is better and safer that governors should be compelled to submit to some restraints than that absolute power should be vested in even the best and ablest and purest of men. The principle of a short ballot is the decrease of elective offices, but not necessarily the placing of absolute and unrestrained power in the hands of one man.

It is quite true that a state constitution should deal only with permanent and fundamental provisions and should not attempt to regulate matters of detail which can be adequately dealt with by ordinary legislation and which are in their nature and operation readily changeable. I am in full accord in this, as in other respects, with the state platform adopted by the Republican party last year and on which the Republican delegates to the Constitutional Convention were elected. Subordinate and non-essential matters of mere regulation and detail ought not to be embodied in constitutions. But I venture to assert that in reason and sound policy there can be no more important, permanent, or fundamental constitutional provision than one relating to the manner of selecting the highest state officers in whom all the executive and administrative powers of our state government are to be vested. This is a subject eminently fit and proper for a constitution to regulate. If this convention cannot solve the problem of establishing a sound system of nomination for elective state offices, at least in outline and cardinal features, no legislature can be expected to do so. In any event, the new Constitution should emphatically declare that the right peaceably to assemble in a political convention composed of duly elected delegates or representatives for the purpose of nominating candidates for public office, state or local, should not be abridged, as it is abridged by the present Election Law.

I further venture to assert that the question of nominating candidates by delegate conventions involves in its essence the perpetuation of the fundamental principles of representative government and of the republican form of government which the founders intended to establish and to guarantee to each state of the Union.

The one great contribution which the English-speaking race has made to the science of politics has been the representative principle. It has been truly declared that every lasting liberty secured for the individual, every lasting reform towards stability in government and permanent effectiveness in administration, every lasting advancement made in politics during the past two centuries, has been by and through the representative system. The subordination of public officials to the law, and their liability under the law for every illegal act, sprang from the representative principle. The independence of the judiciary, that great bulwark of liberty and of the rights of the individual, has followed upon the growth and success of the representative principle. The vivifying spirit or essence of the representative principle is the determination of all questions of practical government by delegates or representatives chosen by the people, who it is assumed can act more intelligently and better discern the true interests of their country than a multitude of voters dispersed over an extensive territory. Government under the representative principle includes not merely legislation by the chosen representatives of the people, but the practical conduct of the executive department and its administrative branches by officials selected or nominated by representatives of the people. Despite all attacks upon our political institutions and all instances of mistakes and maladministration, the sound common sense of thoughtful citizens still confirms the judgment of the founders of our government that the only safe course is to follow the representative principle. This is as true to-day as it was when the " Federalist " was written. The direct nomination of executive or judicial officers is in utter disregard of that principle.

If the function of legislation is in the long run most satisfactorily performed by a representative body composed of men from every locality and every part of a state, and if it would be unsafe to vest the lawmaking power in the executive branch, does it not likewise follow that the equally important function of selecting candidates for executive and judicial office and formulating party policies and platforms will be better performed by a representative body, such as delegate conventions, than by being left to the mass of voters? If more intelligent legislation and wiser action are likely to result from a representative body than from the confusion of a multitude of voters, is it not also evident that more intelligent and discriminating selection of executive officers will be made by chosen representatives, as in nominating conventions, than by the people at large?

It should be borne in mind that our system of republican government differs from other representative governments in the practical and effective separation of powers. In England and in France the legislators, that is the delegates or representatives elected by the people, appoint and control all executive and administrative officers and carry on the executive and administrative branches of government. There the legislative and executive powers are practically united in the same body. Under our system the legislators do not elect or appoint executive officers. It is, therefore, essential, as I am profoundly convinced, that executive officers should be nominated by duly qualified representatives if the representative principle is to be maintained.

Nomination of executive officers by direct primaries will inevitably be subversive of the true spirit of the representative system, and the secrecy of the vote in the nominating primaries will ultimately be destructive of all sense of responsibility. The enrolled voter marking his ballot in secret will frequently feel no sense of responsibility or accountability to his neighbors and fellow-citizens, and will frequently fail to appreciate that his vote is a sacred trust to be exercised for the good of the community. The secrecy of the primary vote thus does a great moral mischief in destroying the sense of political responsibility and accountability. A public declaration in connection with nominations for office, involving as it does a recommendation to other voters of fitness and qualification for the particular office, is a much more effective restraint on corruption and perversion of the popular vote than any scheme of secrecy which leaves no one publicly responsible for unfit and improper nominations. In my judgment, the primary system tends to promote the nomination of self-advertisers, demagogues and wire-pullers by irresponsible minorities, groups, factions, cabals, or secret societies, generally

composed of persons acting in the dark and dominated or controlled by leaders who cannot be held to
any accountability, however much they may abuse
or prostitute the political power they exercise.

The nomination of candidates for public office,
whether national, state, or local, by means of party
conventions, caucuses, or conferences, was introduced and long existed without any statutory
regulation. The practice sprang up normally and
from necessity as soon as the increase of population
rendered it impracticable for the voters to come
together in mass or town meeting. The body of
voters, who could not spend the time necessary to
investigate as to the qualifications of candidates,
or attend political debates, and who could know
little or nothing of the competency and character
of candidates, naturally recognized that the best
and safest course would be to elect delegates or
representatives from each neighborhood, who, meeting delegates or representatives from other districts,
could exchange views, criticize, discuss and agree
upon policies and nominations, and thus act more
intelligently, advisedly and wisely than would otherwise be possible.

The growth of constituencies, the multiplication
of elective offices, and the neglect of their political
duties by the majority of electors led to many abuses
in the management of nominating conventions, and
legislation became necessary in order to prevent
frauds in connection with the conduct of primaries
and conventions. In promoting this legislation, it was

argued that, if citizens were assured the right to be
enrolled in the party to which they desired to belong
and to vote at primaries and freely to exercise their
choice for delegates to conventions, they would be
stimulated to take part in the primaries, and that
this would result in preventing party nominations
for office from being controlled by those who made
politics their business or used improper or corrupt
methods.   Hence the primary reform measures introduced by legislation in our state in the nineties.

These measures, however, proved to be sadly
disappointing to many of their promoters.   This was
not because the statutes were in themselves defective
or inadequate, but because it was found to be impossible by mere legislative enactment to induce a
majority of the electors to enroll in their parties or
to take any active part or interest in politics.
Although under these primary laws the nominating
conventions could at any time have been readily
controlled by the electorate at large, had the voters
only taken the trouble to enroll and vote at the
primaries, great dissatisfaction arose or was fomented
or manufactured, and a demand created for the total
abolition of the convention and the introduction of
the experiment of a direct primary system, upon the
notion that this would stimulate greater political
interest, enable the enrolled voters to control and
elect their own candidates, bring nominations closer
to the people, and curtail and ultimately destroy
the power of the politicians and bosses.   The new
experiment was based upon the assumption that

if enrolled electors could vote directly for candidates instead of for representatives to nominating conventions, they would thereby be induced to take a more active interest in politics, to overthrow the control or domination of bosses and professional politicians, and to make better selections than had ever been made before.   In a word, it was assumed in the face of all experience to the contrary that, if the voters had the direct power, they would perform their political duties, that better qualified and more competent and independent candidates would offer themselves or somehow would be brought to the attention of the electorate, and that nominations would then represent the will or choice of the majority in each party, and not the will of minorities, or the choice of bosses.   How the majority were to ascertain the qualifications of particular candidates or cooperate to secure the nomination of the best qualified was left in the air.   It seemed to be thought, following the absurd and exploded doctrines of Rousseau, that the people would always want and, by a process of political inspiration, would intuitively and instinctively select, the best men for public office.

The result so far has refuted all these assumptions, hopes and promises. The people at large do not take part in the primaries, and the political machines are more powerful than ever.   Thus, in New York county, the Republican vote for governor at the direct primaries of 1914 was only 23,305, out of a total enrollment of 56,108 and a vote in November of 85,478; the Democratic primary vote was only 48,673 out of a total enrollment of 132,693 and a vote in November of 90,666, and the Progressive primary vote was only 6,972 out of a total enrollment of 19,705 and a vote in November of 5,604. It will be readily perceived from these figures that a small minority of the voters in each party took the trouble to participate in the direct primary elections, even in the case of the nomination for governor of our state, as to which there was an exciting contest in each party. An examination of the figures throughout the entire state will show that the voters in nearly all districts took less interest in direct primary elections for nominations than they were accustomed to take under the old convention system and that the controlling power is still being exercised by the organization, but now acting in secret and utterly irresponsible. For example, the Republican primary vote for governor in Bronx county was 5,276 against a Republican vote of 29,865 in November, and in Richmond county the Republican primary vote for governor was 984 against a Republican vote of 5,477 in November. It is probably correct to assume that not one-half of the Republican or Democratic voters now enroll, and that, on an average, less than one-half of the enrolled voters take the trouble to go to the primaries, even when there is a serious contest, as was the case last year for governor. There were then three proposed Republican candidates, Whitman, Hedges and Hinman, and the result was that less than one-sixth of the Republican vote in November might have been sufficient to carry the primaries, the total Republican vote for governor having been 686,701 as against a total primary vote of 226,037 for the three candidates. Under the present direct primaries, the voters of a small portion of the state can put a candidate in nomination by petition; any number of names may be put on the official primary ballot, and a candidate may be put in nomination by a very small minority vote confined to a single locality.   In fact, twenty or more names can be placed by petition on the official primary ballot of any party as candidates for any elective office, and the name of the person receiving the largest number of votes will be that of the candidate of a great party, to whose support the party will be committed and for whose conduct in office the party will be responsible, although the successful candidate may be entirely unknown to nineteen-twentieths of the voters at that particular primary. Under the present primary system, in view of the small number of those participating in primaries, an insignificant percentage of the voters at a primary could nominate a candidate of whose qualifications and personal character the majority of the party were wholly ignorant, or a candidate whom an overwhelming majority would utterly repudiate. Sulzer came very near carrying the direct primary of the Progressive party. This shows how readily the direct primary system engenders factions and irresponsibility, and how unfit it is for securing the expression of the intelligent and instructed will of the majority of any party. Moreover, there is no way of ascertaining for whom petitions are being circulated; no publicity is required even after the time for filing petitions, and the great majority of enrolled voters generally have no idea of the candidates for office on the official primary ballot until they open the official ballots at their polling-places. The press is either uninterested or partisan, and it fails adequately to discuss the qualifications and character of candidates.

I submit that it is absurd to claim that such a method of nominating state officers to administer government for a population of over 10,000,000 is more likely to secure competent and trustworthy candidates, or to express the real preference and the sober and intelligent judgment of the majority of the voters of each party, than the old method of nominating state officers by public conventions composed of delegates and representatives of the voters from each assembly or election district of the state, proceeding in the open with full opportunity for investigation, discussion and criticism.

The conventions of the two great political parties held at Saratoga last year, at which the party platforms in respect of the approaching Constitutional Convention were adopted and fifteen delegates-at-large "recommended," were wholly unofficial and unregulated by law. What was practically the nomination by the conventions of candidates for delegates-at-large was unauthorized and operated only as a mere recommendation. They had to be nominated by petition as fully as if the conventions had never met. These conventions thus nominated delegates because they realized, and every thinking man in the state appreciated, that it would be preposterous to leave the selection and nomination of fifteen delegates-at-large to the mass of enrolled voters who would have no opportunity for conference and exchange of views in respect of the qualifications and character of the candidates. Some informed, responsible and representative body of men had to act, and therefore the conventions acted — in the very teeth of the law. They, however, refrained from considering candidates for the great office of governor, on the theory that it would be violating the spirit and intent of the Election Law to take any action in regard to candidates for that office! What inconsistency! The most important and vital subject of the governorship was left to the hazard of petitions circulated among the enrolled voters throughout the state. There were no organizations of any kind among the voters, except what are known as the political organizations, and no other means of communication and exchange of views or debate. Of course, it was confidently anticipated that the organization in each party would determine, or at least would have it within its power to determine, who should be the candidates of that party. Such proved to be the case. No candidate was nominated at the direct primaries for a state office unless he was supported by the regular organization or machine of his party. And that, I believe, will be the practical result of direct primaries in nine cases out of ten, and more readily and frequently and unsatisfactorily than under the old convention system.

Careful observers of the operation of the primary law last year in this state, and for several years in other states, have become convinced that the result of this so-called reform has been not only to increase the power of the regular organization or machine but to render it utterly irresponsible. The organization now acts in secret behind closed doors and without accountability to any one except its own inner circle. The leaders have only to whisper their orders over the telephone to the workers in each district, preserving no record, and the desired result is accomplished. If an unfit and improper nomination is made, the leaders can disclaim all responsibility and say that such is the will of the sovereign people. As the vote at the primary is secret, no one can be blamed; there is no individual or group of individuals upon whom responsibility can ever be fastened. If it be argued that there is actual responsibility and that everyone knows it, then I answer that this is only by admitting that, after all, the secret machine or boss is in fact responsible and still rules, and now more effectively than ever.

As has been pointed out by many able writers, the convention system in the past has been of inestimable service to this country. With all its vagaries, it afforded the highest test of a political representative institution in a democratic community and the soundest and purest application of the principle of representation or delegated authority; it operated to bind party elements firmly together; it afforded full opportunity for exchange of views, criticism and debate, for the propagation of principles, for the conciliation of factions; it inspired enthusiastic party life. The convention, if honestly conducted, was a thoroughly representative and deliberative body, and it was the true cause of party success and of the maintenance and perpetuation of party principles and policies, as well as political faith and devotion. In a word, the convention was and still is the best instrument ever devised for securing concert of choice and responsible and intelligent action by large bodies of voters belonging to the same political party and believing in the same political faith, principles and policies.

I am not at all blind to the fact that there have been great abuses in the convention system, and that conventions have been at times corruptly organized or conducted. But I know of no form of abuse or corruption which could not have been remedied by appropriate and intelligent legislation, or which could not have been prevented in New York by action of the voters if the legislation of the past twenty-five years had been generally availed of by the majority in each party. The control of all nominations was in the hands of the majority, if they had only taken the trouble to enroll and vote for competent representatives at primary elections. There is no practical remedy for abuse of power, fraud, or corruption in nominations for office but the participation in politics of all voters as a duty of citizenship. The notion that the direct primary would eliminate the professional politician and the boss has been shown to be false in every state where the scheme has been tried. Indeed, quite the contrary has been the result, and the last condition is worse than the first; for, to repeat myself, manipulators, wire-pullers and political bosses now work in secret and by underground channels without any responsibility or accountability whatever, and are, nevertheless, able cynically to point to the direct primary as the expression of the people's sovereign will — a primary which may be carried by a very small minority of the party.

I assume that all the members of this Constitutional Convention believe that the existence of political parties is essential to the success of free government and to permanence and stability of political policy, and that the perpetuation of party government is desirable for the welfare and best interests of this state. Men cannot secure results and compass their ends in politics, any more than in most other human concerns and matters requiring concerted action, except by organization, cooperation, discipline and responsibility. The value of the service rendered to the American people by the great political parties is incalculable, and if these parties are to be disrupted and their organization and cohesiveness undermined, the result must inevitably be a most serious injury to the body politic. Whether we regard political parties, on the one hand, as organizations of men believing in the same political faith, principles and policies and uniting to introduce or uphold those principles and policies, or, on the other hand, merely as organizations to secure office and administer government — both of which aspects present patriotic motives — it is desirable for the permanent welfare of the people of every free country that parties should be maintained, and particularly that there should be two great responsible parties, each striving for control and ready to assume the responsibility of government and of the adoption of particular measures. A public official who belongs to a great political party and owes his preferment to that party is under a double sense of responsibility for efficiency, honesty and consistency in public office. He has a sense of responsibility and duty to the state as a whole, and he has a sense of responsibility and duty to his party, and both are moral factors of inestimable worth in securing integrity, efficiency and industry in public office.

In its real origin, the movement to abolish the convention system and introduce direct nominating primaries sprang not from any hope of reforming the existing political parties but from a desire to subvert and destroy the American system of government by political parties. The scheme was later taken up by men who sincerely desired to reform party management and correct party abuses, who conscientiously despaired of reform within the parties themselves, and who conceived and finally came to believe that betterment could be brought about only by uprooting and casting aside all the party machinery, organization and discipline which had been built up by the practical experience of over a century. The plea of bringing the government back to the people was catching and plausible, and it found eager response in the deeply rooted dislike of party machinery, party discipline and party constancy on the part of those who habitually neglect all attention to politics and the political duties of citizenship except during periods of popular excitement and upheaval.

Although I am one of those who believe in independence in politics and in the right and duty of every citizen to vote against his party if in his judgment the public interests so require, I profoundly believe that party government and party organization and machinery are absolutely essential under our form of government. Political parties in America have given stability to governmental policies and have created the only effective restraint upon disintegration and individual caprice or demagogism. There must be coherence in political forces; there must be concentration and direction of the political energy of communities; there must be some systematic and practical method of investigating the qualifications of candidates and selecting competent public officials; there must be stability, harmony and cooperation in governmental policies. These can be secured in the long run only by and through permanently organized and disciplined political parties. No other method has yet been discovered by which effectively to express political opinion, to secure stability in governmental administration and policies, and to effectuate the real and permanent judgment of the people and promote their best interests.

President Wilson some years ago, in referring to attacks upon party government in the United States, used the following striking language, which I think should be now recalled:

"I know that it has been proposed by enthusiastic, but not too practical, reformers to do away with parties by some legerdemain of governmental reconstruction, accompanied and supplemented by some rehabilitation, devoutly to be wished, of the virtues least commonly controlling in fallen human nature; but it seems to me that it would be more difficult and less desirable than these amiable persons suppose to conduct a government of the many by means of any other device than party organization, and that the great need is, not to get rid of parties, but to find and use some expedient by which they can be managed and made amenable from day to day to public opinion." "Whatever their faults and abuses, party machines are absolutely necessary under our existing electoral arrangements, and are necessary chiefly for keeping the several segments of parties together. . . . It is important to keep this in mind. Otherwise, when we analyze party action, we shall fall into the too common error of thinking that we are analyzing disease. As a matter of fact the whole thing is just as normal and natural as any other political development. The part that party has played in this country has been both necessary and beneficial, and if bosses and secret managers are often undesirable persons, playing their parts for their own benefit or glorification rather than for the public good, they are at least the natural fruits of the tree. It has borne fruit good and bad, sweet and bitter, wholesome and corrupt, but it is native to our air and practice and can be uprooted only by an entire change of system."[1]

For these reasons I earnestly urge upon the Constitutional Convention of the state of New York the restoration of nominating state conventions for elective state offices. I do so because I believe that they are the best means of maintaining political parties, of formulating their principles and policies, of purifying and disciplining their management, of stimulating political enthusiasm and disinterestedness, and of selecting and nominating fit and representative individuals as candidates for high public office. I further urge that the nominees of any such convention should not need any further designation than the filing of a certificate by the proper convention officers. If it be concluded, however, that the direct primary system should be continued for the purpose of party nominations, then it should be provided that the name of the nominee of the convention should be placed on

---

[1] Congressional Government, p. 97, and Constitutional Government in the United States, pp. 209, 210.

the official primary ballot with the designation "nominated by convention." This would enable the enrolled voters to ratify or overrule the action of their convention. I am, however, convinced that this nominating primary would impose an unnecessary burden upon the electorate, and that it would be a mistake to increase the number of elections. We should then have three elections: first, the election of delegates to the nominating convention; second, the official primaries, and third, the general election. It seems to me that it would answer every purpose if adequate provision were retained for independent nominations by petition and if nominating primaries were dispensed with. This would enable voters belonging to any party to place candidates in the field in opposition to the nominees of the convention if they were dissatisfied with those nominees.

Assuming that we are to continue the system of electing judges to our highest judicial offices, that is, judges of the Court of Appeals and justices of the Supreme Court, then I submit that candidates for these very important offices should be nominated by conventions and not by direct primaries. I regard this as even more essential in the case of nomination for judicial office than in the case of nomination for executive office.

The qualities required in a candidate for high judicial office are knowledge of the law, love of justice, high personal character, calmness, impartiality and independence. Mere popularity, or what so often is necessary to popularity, good-fellowship,

is the last quality we look for in a judge. The
self-seeker and self-advertiser is seldom qualified by
temperament or character for judicial office. It
requires the most thorough investigation as to the
professional learning, career and conduct of a candidate and the most sifting exchange of views before
a judicial candidate can be intelligently and wisely
selected. For want of adequate means of acquir-
ing information, the public in such large constituencies as the whole state of New York (in the case
of judges of the Court of Appeals) and the various
judicial districts (in the case of justices of the Supreme Court) cannot intelligently estimate the
qualifications of judicial candidates. It seems to
me nonsense to argue that in parties composed
of hundreds of thousands of enrolled electors
dispersed throughout the state, the voters can
investigate, or exchange views, or intelligently act
in regard to the qualifications of lawyers who are
proposed as candidates for judicial office — almost
as preposterous as if we were to select judicial
candidates by lot from the names placed on the
official primary list.

The test of fitness for judicial office should in-
disputably be higher and more technical than for
other offices. That test should require special
capacity and character, to be ascertained by careful
investigation, exchange of views, open discussion
and comparison of merits by responsible delegates
or representatives charged with that particular duty
and acting in public and personally accountable for

mistake, perversion, or corruption. This test can be best secured by the convention system; practically it cannot be secured at all by any system of secret direct primaries.

Reform in the selection of judges, if their selection is to be by election, lies not in schemes to reform human nature by legislative nostrums and to destroy publicity and responsibility, but in making the voters appreciate that the government is theirs, that political power is theirs, that theirs is the duty to send competent representatives to conventions, that theirs is the responsibility of electing competent men, and that they are vitally interested in having a competent, impartial and independent judiciary. Political conventions will be reliable and responsive if the people will only see to it that competent, honest and patriotic men are elected to represent them. There is no other course unless we uproot our whole system of republican government.

Ten years of experimenting with our Election Law have produced the present hodge-podge under which no election is conducted without error and without inviting a lawsuit and from which all but experts and professional politicians turn away in irritation and disgust. The net result has been to complicate our elections and make them less and less responsive to the best public opinion, and more and more subject to the control of professional politicians, wire-pullers and bosses.

In conclusion, though repeating myself, I earnestly submit that there can be no greater menace to our

political institutions and to government by the
people than the prevailing tendency to weaken and
impair the representative principle in our state governments by nominating executive and judicial
officers through direct secret primaries instead of
through public conventions composed of delegates
or representatives duly chosen by the enrolled voters
of the parties and charged with the duty of selecting
competent and honest candidates and directly accountable to the locality they represent for the failure to perform that duty. These delegates represent
the people of the various districts of the state; they
come together in public; they exchange and discuss
views, or at any rate have full opportunity for debate
and criticism; they vote in public for this or that
candidate, and then they return to their neighbors, to
those who sent them and for whom they spoke and
voted, and face accountability and responsibility.
Is not such a proceeding much more likely to secure
competent and honest candidates than the present
system of leaving the voter at large to slip into a
dimly lighted booth and secretly place a cross on
an unidentifiable ballot? The convention system
is sound and should be preserved; it alone will perpetuate our parties and our form of government, and
in casting the representative principle aside, as is
necessarily done in the direct primary system of
nominations for state and judicial office, we are beginning a process which, if not checked, will end in
what Lincoln called political suicide.

CATHOLIC PAROCHIAL SCHOOLS[1]

THE completion of this building, its dedication to education, and the opening of its doors as a Catholic parochial school are matters of no ordinary significance in this community. By means of the present function we are publicly emphasizing the religious character of the educational work to be undertaken here. Due respect for the opinion of our neighbors and fellow-citizens seems to call for some statement from the standpoint of the Catholic laity in explanation of the reasons which have impelled a comparatively poor congregation to incur this great expense and to assume an obligation of future maintenance which year after year will constitute a very serious and increasing burden. It is indeed a striking event that a congregation, very few of whom have large means, should have erected and equipped such a building, costing over $150,000, and should have pledged itself to support the school and ultimately to discharge the remaining mortgage indebtedness of $50,000.

There is unfortunately much misunderstanding and criticism among our fellow-citizens of other denominations in regard to the attitude of the Roman

[1] Remarks at the dedication of the Roman Catholic parochial school at Glen Cove, Long Island, New York, on September 6, 1915.

Catholic Church towards the important and far-reaching subject of the education of children in the public schools, and the Catholic point of view is frequently misrepresented.

In the first place, it is constantly asserted that Catholics are opposed to the public school system of America. On the contrary, Catholics approve and support the public schools, and willingly vote and pay their share of the taxes necessary for the maintenance of these schools. They believe that the state should provide free common schools for the education of children, so that every American child not only shall have an opportunity of securing a free education but may be compelled to take advantage of the opportunity thus provided. They recognize that in this country it is generally impracticable in the common schools to teach the tenets of religious faiths, because to compel children indiscriminately to study the doctrines of any particular religion in which their parents do not believe would destroy all religious freedom and would be contrary to fundamental rights. They recognize further that to attempt to teach in the public schools the tenets of the Catholic, the Jewish and the numerous Protestant denominations, would be quite impossible and inevitably would lead to religious chaos. They realize that absolute equality or religious freedom can be secured only by making the public schools non-sectarian. Catholics, therefore, favor the maintenance of the system of free common schools; they have heretofore supported and will

continue to support the system, although they
object to some of the details of management, and
they will send and do send their children to these
public schools wherever there are no Catholic schools.
In fact, fully one-half of the Catholic children of our
country are now attending public schools because of
the lack of Catholic schools.

Thousands of well-to-do Protestants and Jews —
many in our own immediate neighborhood — send
their children to private schools, whether day or
boarding schools, in many of which the Protestant
faith is taught. Yet no one suggests that, because
these parents send their children to private schools,
they are in any sense acting in hostility to the public
schools, or to American institutions, or to the best interests of their own children. As parents, they have
and ought to have the right to send their children
to such schools as they think will afford them
an education more complete and more conducive
to the formation of moral character than they
can secure at the public schools. Catholics are but
exercising the same common right, and what, moreover, they believe to be their duty as parents, when
they send their children to the parochial schools
which are erected, equipped and maintained at their
own expense.

Another misrepresentation, and one which Catholics resent, is the statement that the parochial and
other Catholic schools do not inculcate patriotism,
and that they teach anti-American doctrines. Any
candid investigator will readily find that this charge

is wholly unfounded. In Catholic schools, 'patriotism, obedience to the law and loyalty to the Constitution are taught as a religious even more than a civic duty; the best and highest ideals of American patriotism and citizenship are exalted. No true American Catholic can be other than a good and patriotic American citizen. Children are taught in these schools that loyal obedience to the laws and religious tolerance are the two essential elements of good Catholic citizenship, and in every form and aspect they are impressed with the obligation as a religious duty to render unto Cæsar the things which are Cæsar's and unto God the things which are God's and to be ever thankful that in this country these two separate obligations are wholly reconcilable.

The fundamental and controlling reason or motive for the establishment and maintenance of parochial schools is the profound conviction on the part of all Roman Catholics, in which conviction clergy and laity are a unit, that the welfare of the state, the stability of the Union, the continuance of civil and religious freedom, and the lasting happiness of the individual depend upon the code and standards of morality, discipline, self-restraint and temperance taught by religion. The student of history well knows that social order and civilized society have always rested upon religion; that there has never been a civilized nation without religion; that free government has never long endured except in countries where some religious faith has prevailed, and that our own country for three centuries has been

an essentially religious country, by which I mean
that the great majority of citizens have been be-
lievers in God and in some Christian religion. When
the Constitution of the United States was established, the Americans were a truly religious people,
and as a whole held firmly to one form or another
of Christian faith. It has been recently pointed
out by Archbishop Ireland in the Cathedral of St.
Paul that in those days, " to stay away from religious
service on Sunday was to invoke upon one's self
serious public criticism." It is quite true that the
great majority of Americans were then Protestants,
but they were a religious majority. The Catholics
can never forget that they owe the blessing of the
religious liberty and tolerance which they now enjoy to a generation that was overwhelmingly Protestant and that it was first granted at an epoch
when religious liberty and tolerance were practically
unknown in Europe, whether in Catholic or Protestant countries.

Lord Bryce in his great work on "The American
Commonwealth" has reviewed the influence of religion in this country, and has declared that "one is
startled by the thought of what might befall this
huge yet delicate fabric of laws and commerce and
social institutions were the foundation it has rested
upon to crumble away." That foundation he recognized to be religion, and he admonished us that "the
more democratic republics become, the more the
masses grow conscious of their own power, the more
do they need to live, not only by patriotism, but by

reverence and self-control, and the more essential to
their well-being are those sources whence reverence
and self-control flow."[1]   Catholics believe that those
sources of reverence and self-control are to be found
in religion, and that if we sow in irreligion we shall
reap in irreligion. Hence the firm and uncompromising determination of Catholic clergy and laity
that thorough and efficient religious instruction, so
far as lies in their power, shall be a vital and essential element in the education of every American
Catholic child.

I very much doubt whether any respectable number of sensible and reflecting American citizens in our
day would challenge the truth that morality is essential to the maintenance of civilized society and government, that the greatest influence for morality is
to be found in the churches of the various denominations throughout the country, and that in teaching
morality the churches are rendering a patriotic service and promoting the best interests and the highest
policy of the state.   I venture to assert that the
only reasonable difference of opinion possible among
candid and just men is as to the best way of incul-
cating religion in the young and the extent to which
religious instruction is essential as a part of the
complete education of children.   On the one hand,
there are those who conscientiously assert and sincerely believe that their children can receive all the
religious training they need at home or at Sunday
school and that they do not require any religious

[1] The American Commonwealth, new edition (1912), vol. II, pp. 793, 794.

instruction in the daily schoolroom; on the other hand, there are those who conscientiously assert and sincerely believe that religion is the most essential part of the education of the child and of the forming of its moral character, that few parents have the time or the ability to teach religion to their children, and that religion can properly be taught only by making it part and parcel of the early schoolroom and of every day's instruction and study, while the mind and character of the child are plastic. The latter view is that of Catholics and of constantly increasing numbers of Protestants who send their children to private schools in which the doctrines of their faith are taught.

In the Catholic view, the influence of the school upon the future manhood and womanhood and citizenship of the country cannot be over-estimated. The school is the nursery where the mind and heart of the impressionable child are moulded into enduring form; the subtle influence of daily religious surroundings, including example and suggestion in the classroom, is as strong and pervading as it is difficult to analyze; the lessons of the primary and elementary school are those that endure and in time dominate the child's mind; and the visible examples of daily discipline, uniformity of ideals, obedience, self-control and disinterested devotedness to Church and country, indeed the very atmosphere of the Catholic religious school, are of themselves formative and educative elements. It is the classroom that is the training field of character and good citizenship — of true manhood and womanhood. Yet many would wholly exclude and banish its most important and essential feature!

Catholics believe that religion and the philosophy of Christianity are not to be taught haphazard, at odd moments, or by untrained persons, and that a firm grasp of the truths of the Catholic religion — or in fact of any religion — by the immature minds and hearts of children cannot be secured by merely reciting abstract maxims of morality, or without constant example and precept, daily lessons, long training and thorough drilling. They further believe that, except in rare instances, this cannot be done by home instruction or by attendance at Sunday school once a week. The immense sacrifices that Catholics have made and are making all over the country ought to demonstrate how sincere is their conviction upon this point. We may form some idea of the extent of this sacrifice from this building and from the fact that the assessed valuation of the Catholic parochial schools in the city of New York is now over $30,000,000.

The story of the heroic struggles and sacrifices of Catholics in order to maintain their system of schools for the education of their children ought to be known to every American Catholic, for it is the most thrilling and inspiring page in the history of their church. The time remaining to me will permit only a brief review of the results accomplished. It is an accomplishment of which Catholics may justly feel proud.

The greatest single religious fact in the United

States to-day is undoubtedly the Catholic school system maintained by private individuals. The Catholic parish schools now number over 5,000, and the academies and colleges over 900, with over 1,500,000 pupils in attendance at these schools and colleges. More than 20,000 Catholic men and women unselfishly devote their lives to the work of teaching in these schools, academies and colleges. The system is crowned by a great Catholic university at Washington with an attendance of nearly 1,500. This vast educational organization is maintained at a yearly cost of millions of dollars without any public aid whatever, except the exemption of school property from ordinary taxation. The efficiency of the Catholic schools and colleges has long been demonstrated by examinations and practical results, and it is at last generally conceded. The Catholic schools teach everything that is taught in the public schools and, in addition, they teach religion and religious morality. The standards of education in all secular branches are equal and in many instances superior to those of the neighborhood public or private schools. In other words, Catholic children are as well educated in the Catholic schools as in the public schools; they come from them as well trained and as patriotic as the children coming from any other schools, and in addition they are thoroughly grounded in the doctrines of their great religion. I say "great" because it is the great religion of all Christendom as well as of this country. When the Constitution of the

United States was framed at the Philadelphia convention of 1787, there were only about 25,000 avowed
Catholics in the whole Union. To-day they number
17,000,000. More than one-third of all who now
attend Christian churches in the United States are
Roman Catholics. The Catholic Church has several
times as many members as any other religious denomination. The figures in the state of New York
show that about 65 per cent., nearly two-thirds, of all
regular attendants at Christian churches, are Roman
Catholics, and that the remaining attendants are
divided among many separate Protestant denominations. Hence the correctness of the assertion that
the Catholic religion is the great religion of this
country.

It is true and should be added that Catholics
hope that the day will come when the people of
all denominations will more adequately appreciate
the fact that religious instruction tends to promote the best and the most loyal citizenship, that
the Catholic parochial schools are, therefore, rendering a public service, and that as such they should be
allotted a reasonable part of the public educational
fund raised from general taxation, measured by and
limited to the actual saving to that fund, provided
also that a required standard of education be maintained. In England, for example, the Catholic parochial schools receive grants of public moneys if they
fulfil certain conditions of efficiency in secular instruction, staff qualification and equipment, and the extent
of these grants is approximately the actual saving

to the public fund. In the Catholic diocese of Long
Island, in which we live, there are now over 68,000
children being educated in the Catholic schools and
colleges, and in Greater New York there are more
than 130,000 children attending the parochial schools.
All these children would have to be educated in the
public schools and at the expense of the taxpayers
if the Catholic schools did not educate them, and this
Catholic education involves an immense direct saving to the public school fund. Statistics recently submitted to the Constitutional Convention sitting at
Albany showed that the immediate saving to the
city of New York alone from the parochial schools
was fully $7,500,000 per annum, and that not one
penny of this saving was being contributed by the
city or the state to the cost of educating and training these Catholic children. Consequently, it is
not unreasonable to believe that justice and tolerance will finally prevail, and that the day will come
when it will be recognized as equitable and as a wise
and enlightened public policy to provide that whenever any denomination, whether Catholic, Protestant,
or Jewish, is, in addition to giving religious instruction, educating and training large numbers of children
according to satisfactory secular standards and
tests, and is thereby relieving the public educational
fund, every such denominational school should be
granted out of the public funds some part of the
actual saving so made, because it is rendering a
public service. A basis of adjustment will, I am
confident, be ultimately worked out, which will be

fair and just to all denominations. But in the meantime the private schools where both secular and religious training are given to children, including the Catholic parochial schools, must continue to be erected, equipped and supported wholly by the members of the various denominations. There are now numerous Protestant private schools where the Protestant faith is being taught; and what is true of the Catholic parochial schools is also true of the Protestant schools.

We are all so accustomed to the blessings of absolute religious liberty that we really find it difficult to imagine that any other condition could ever have been tolerated in the free air of America, and we are very apt to overlook or minimize the value of the most precious privilege we enjoy. Yet, it is only a few generations since religious intolerance prevailed in the United States and Catholics were mercilessly and barbarously persecuted. The first constitution of the state of New York in 1777 discriminated against Catholics by permitting only Protestants to become citizens of the state, and this was done notwithstanding the fact that the Continental Congress had three years before entreated the states to bury religious intolerance forever in oblivion. At one time in the colony of New York Catholic priests were hunted as criminals, were condemned to perpetual imprisonment if apprehended, and were to suffer the death penalty if they broke prison and were retaken. Catholics could not hold civil or military positions, and could not even worship God ac-

cording to their faith without becoming criminals
and liable to imprisonment. The only period of full
religious tolerance and liberty in our colonial history
was for a short time during the term of Governor
Dongan, who was a Roman Catholic.

All this intolerance has happily passed away never
to return, and religious liberty is now firmly established. I recall the past only in order to impress
upon your minds that we should treasure this blessing and be ever grateful to the generation of Americans, overwhelmingly Protestant, which gave us
religious freedom and in doing so went far toward
atoning for the past persecution of Catholics.

In conclusion, I must add that we Catholics of the
Parish of St. Patrick of Glen Cove should acclaim
our appreciation of the great service and unselfish
devotion of the one person whose whole-hearted
energy has made this school possible and without
whose example we should despair of maintaining it.
Long may this beautiful building endure as a splendid
monument to the faith and patriotism of a Catholic
priest, our beloved pastor, Bernard O'Reilly. We
must also voice our cordial welcome and pledge of
support to the Sisters of Notre Dame, worthy members of a great American Catholic sisterhood devoted to the education of children, who are now
about to take up among us the task of teaching our
children. They will labor week after week and year
after year, devotedly and unselfishly, for a pittance
barely sufficient to supply their absolute physical
needs, with little or no expectation of public recog-

nition. They will seek and find their reward solely in the inward satisfaction of the day's work and duty well done and in the inspiring and quickening maxim of their order and of their whole daily life that their holy task is ever

PRO DEO ET ECCLESIA ET PATRIA.

THE FRANCE–AMERICA COMMITTEE OF NEW YORK [1]

I ASK you, Gentlemen, to rise and lift your glasses high to the joint toast of his Excellency the President of the United States, his Excellency the President of the Republic of France and his Majesty the King of England.

I ask you again to rise and lift your glasses high to the joint toast of the other Allies: to his Majesty the King of the Belgians, whose valiant and heroic people have suffered frightfully and have again shown, as Cæsar taught us, that "*horum omnium fortissimi sunt Belgae;*" to his Imperial Majesty the Czar of all the Russias, whose brave soldiers have stood so much of the brunt of the battle and paid such an awful toll, and to his Majesty the King of Italy, and his courageous army and navy, whose help may yet prove decisive.

As the permanent object of the France-America Committee, which was organized long before the present war, is to perpetuate the traditions and bonds of friendship which bind the governments and peoples of France and America together, our guests will

---

[1] Remarks as presiding officer at a luncheon given in honor of the members of the Anglo-French Credit and Finance Commission, at the Hotel Knickerbocker, New York, October 1, 1915.

readily appreciate why France should seem, at the moment, to be foremost in our thoughts.

Monsieur Homberg, Monsieur Mallet: Le Comité France-Amérique de New York éprouve un très vif plaisir à saluer en vous les délégués de la République Française. Le Comité tient à vous témoigner l'amitié des Américains pour la France, notre admiration de l'héroïsme que le peuple français de toutes classes a montré pendant l'année affreuse qui vient de s'écouler, nos ardentes sympathies pour vos souffrances, et nos souhaits pour votre avenir.

Notre hospitalité est malheureusement imprégnée d'une tristesse poignante, car un souci de tous les instants ne nous permet pas d'oublier la guerre brutale et féroce qui a dévasté une grande partie de la France et presque toute la Belgique, et qui menace non seulement les libertés des peuples français et belge, mais la civilisation de toute l'Europe. Il est vrai que notre gouvernement national, pour des raisons d'état, se trouve forcé de maintenir une neutralité légale, tâche si difficile et si complexe, mais le peuple américain ne saurait être indifférent aux malheurs et aux détresses des Français. Un grand Americain a bien dit que c'est en apprenant l'histoire de son pays que l'enfant américain apprend à aimer la France. Nous ne pourrions jamais oublier l'aide généreuse, la sympathie, le dévouement, et le désintéressement que le peuple français nous a témoignés au début de notre histoire. Le souvenir, Messieurs, en est ineffaçable. Innombrables sont mes compatriotes qui prient de tout cœur qu'une nouvelle Bataille de Poitiers contre les Sarrasins délivre bientôt la belle et sainte terre de France de ses envahisseurs.

Le service que la France a rendu aux Etats-Unis est souvent méconnu et quelquefois oublié. L'heure est venue de réfuter et les dénigrements et les préjugés. Le Comité France-Amérique voudrait saisir cette occasion pour rappeler hautement ce que nous devons à la France et exprimer la reconnaissance profonde que le peuple américain ressent envers le peuple français.

La plupart des historiens, cherchant leurs matériaux dans les archives des gouvernements et dans les notes des rois et de leurs ministres, ne voient trop souvent qu'un calcul ou un motif intéressé dans l'aide que la France nous a apportée et dans l'amitié qu'elle nous a témoignée pendant notre Guerre d'Indépendance. Mais ceux qui cherchent consciencieusement à pénétrer jusqu'à l'âme du peuple français pendant les années de 1776 à 1781, comme l'avait fait l'historien Américain, James Breck Perkins, feu le président du Comité des Affaires Etrangères de notre Congrès National, attestent que cette aide, qui fut si efficace et qui seule a rendu notre succès possible, était désinteressée et n'était inspirée que par sympathie pour un peuple faible et par amour pour la liberté et la justice politique. La Fayette, l'ami intime et dévoué de Washington et de Franklin, était véritablement l'incarnation du sentiment d'enthousiasme exalté et de sympathie ardente que· les Français ressentaient alors dans toutes les classes pour un peuple qui voulait être libre. Sans doute

Louis XVI. et Vergennes y voyaient des avantages
incidentels et des raisons d'état, mais c'était bien le
peuple impatient et l'enthousiasme et le sentiment
public de la nation entière qui ont finalement forcé
le gouvernement du Roi à nous envoyer une armée
disciplinée sous Rochambeau et une flotte de guerre
sous d'Estaing et de Grasse. L'importance incalculable du service rendu par les Français peut être
estimée en nous rappelant que les deux tiers et les
mieux équipées des troupes alliées à Yorktown
étaient français, et que ce fut à Rochambeau que le
commandant anglais avait cru devoir rendre son épée.

En prenant part à notre Guerre d'Indépendance,
le peuple français savait parfaitement que son aide
lui coûterait un prix énorme et que les impôts déjà
trop lourds devraient être encore augmentés. L'historien Perkins déclare que le montant des dépenses
de la France pour libérer l'Amérique s'est élevé à sept
cent soixante douze millions de dollars, c'est à dire,
à plus de trois milliards huit cent millions de francs.[1]
De cette énorme dépense, qui a ruiné le trésor
royal, comme l'avait bien prédit Turgot, pas un sou

[1]   France in the American Revolution, p. 498; see also the introduction by Ambassador Jusserand, p. xv. The accuracy of these figures
has not been independently verified.   An examination of the late Mr.
Perkins' papers does not disclose the source of his statement.   The French
archives show a direct expenditure of 1,507,500,000 livres, but these
figures do not include payments made in and after the year 1783.
Professor Marion of the Collège de France is of opinion that the total
expenditure probably reached 2,000,000,000 livres.   Marion, *Histoire
Financière de la France, 1715-1789*, vol. I, p. 303, Paris, 1914; see also
Gomel, *Les Causes Financières de la Révolution Française*, vol. II, p. 36,
Paris, 1893. Fiske, in his   Critical Period,   p. 35, states the expenditure
to have been 1,400,000,000 francs.

n'a été remboursé à la France. Elle ne l'a jamais
réclamé, et elle en refuserait fièrement aujourd'hui
le remboursement en nous rappelant qu'elle avait
stipulé dans le traité d'alliance avec les Etats-Unis
d'Amérique du 6 Février, 1778, qu'elle ne recevrait
aucune indemnité pour sa coopération et ses sacrifices,
et que même si le Canada était conquis, cette contrée
serait annexée aux Etats-Unis et non pas retournée
à la France. Ce traité, sans précédent en générosité
dans l'histoire du monde, était le premier de tous les
traités que les Etats-Unis ont faits et le seul traité
d'alliance dans notre histoire.

Ne serait-il pas souverainement juste, si le peuple
américain, cent trente quatre ans après la bataille
de Yorktown, reconnaissait ce service — je me refuse
à l'appeler dette — en offrant au peuple français un
crédit commercial du principal, c'est à dire, sept
cent soixante douze millions, remboursable quand la
France le pourrait? Même en francs, ce ne serait
que l'équivalent d'une contribution insignifiante
par chaque citoyen des Etats-Unis, et bien moins
en valeur que l'impôt qui a été payé volontaire-
ment et de bon cœur par le peuple français du dix-
huitième siècle pour nous aider. Quelle noblesse,
quelle gloire, quelle splendeur de cœur, d'âme et
d'esprit si les grands banquiers américains avaient
pu proclamer au monde qu'ils avaient eux-mêmes
offert le crédit en reconnaissance du passé! Nous
serions vraiment fiers de notre génération si elle
pouvait écrire une page aussi sublime, aussi impéris-
sable dans l'histoire du monde. Alors, Messieurs,

nul doute ne subsisterait quant au succès éclatant de votre mission, surtout si une parole éloquente pouvait toucher le cœur des Américains et leur rappeler combien ils doivent à la France, à cette république sœur et souffrante, et combien la question aujourd'hui n'est pas seulement une affaire commerciale pour notre propre profit avec nos meilleurs clients, mais aussi une question de gratitude pour un ami loyal et dévoué et de sympathie effective pour un grand et noble peuple qui souffre.

Au nom de cette reconnaissance et de cette sympathie américaines que j'ai essayé d'exprimer en interprétant, j'en suis convaincu, la pensée de tous les Américains réunis ici, je lève mon verre en l'honneur de la République Française, de la France blessée mais si vivante, si courageuse, si valiante, et de ses représentants distingués qui nous honorent de leur présence, M. Octave Homberg et M. Ernest Mallet. Messieurs, j'ai l'honneur de vous présenter M. Homberg.[1]

My Lord Chief Justice of England and Gentlemen of the British Commission: After the eloquent tributes of last night at the Pilgrims, I find it extremely difficult to express and convey to you the full import and sincerity of our welcome.

Every tie that can bind one people to another binds the American people to the English. Most of us are of the Anglo-Saxon race and have the same blood coursing through our veins. To the great majority of Americans, England has ever been the

---

[1] M. Homberg replied in French, and Mr. Guthrie then continued as above.

mother country. We speak the same language, read the same literature, strive for the same ideals, are governed by the same principles of politics and jurisprudence, and entertain the same fundamental conceptions of right and wrong and justice as among men and among nations. The greater part of England's history is our history; her Magna Carta is our Magna Carta, and the immortal deeds of valor of the English, Scotch, Irish and Welsh are our heritage and the source of our inspiration. Our hearts, therefore, cannot but beat faster day after day as we read of the splendid heroism and noble self-sacrifice of your great race.

To our minds the noblest and the most truly glorious page in the history of England was written by Sir Edward Grey when, on behalf of your government, my Lord, he refused to break the plighted faith of England to avoid involving his country in the greatest and most disastrous war in the history of the world, a war for which England was not prepared, for which Sir Edward and his colleagues knew she was not prepared, and which threatened and might involve the ruin of the British Empire. There is a nobility and sublimity, inexpressible by mere words, in the act of sending that small but now immortal British army to Belgium in August of last year, to face tenfold its number, to die for strangers — for a mere "scrap of paper," as a treaty was cynically and immorally called — solely that the honor of England might be kept inviolate. England has never been grander or nobler than on that day. The glory she then gained cannot

fade.   Gentlemen, the Anglo-Saxon race never rose
to higher renown than when the British statesmen
of to-day showed on such a grand scale that the spirit
of the Light Brigade at Balaclava still lives:

> "Their's not to reason why,
> Their's but to do and die."

And we Americans were then prouder than ever
before to belong to the Anglo-Saxon race.

England may prevail in this war, or she may fail.
But whatever may happen, whatever may be decreed by Providence, your magnificent and unselfish
heroism in springing to the defense of Belgium has
added to England's renown and to our race a glory
which is priceless and infinitely beyond the whole
cost of the war, a glory worth dying for, a glory that
will thrill and uplift generations of men for all time,
a glory that will ever inspire acts of patriotic service
and valorous self-sacrifice, of chivalry and honor.

Although, Gentlemen of the British Commission,
the deep sympathy of the great majority of Americans is naturally with the Allies in the present war,
we want you to return to England appreciating why
we must loyally support the neutrality which the
President of the United States has proclaimed.   The
policy of this country in regard to European wars was
fixed in 1793. One of the most important and enduring
of the many services that President Washington rendered to the United States was when he stood firm as
a rock against the abuse and clamor of that day in upholding and enforcing neutrality in favor of England
as against the demands of her then enemies. We have

consistently adhered to that principle for more than one hundred and twenty years. It has been our fixed and constant policy, not a football of politics, or of newspaper propaganda, or of temporary emotion or expediency, but the sober judgment and conscience of the nation. The essence of this policy is that it is the duty of our government, not only to the present but to future generations, to avoid being drawn into European wars unless our honor or our vital interests become involved. During more than a century we have invited the inhabitants of every nation of Europe to come here and become a part of our country, and we have impliedly assured them of our adherence to this traditional policy of neutrality. If, now, we also should draw the sword, out of heartfelt sympathy and friendship for the Allies, or in indignation at the outrage of the violation of Belgium, we might become hereafter constantly involved in European conflicts in which we should have no other than a humanitarian interest, and as a result find the devoted friends and relatives of to-day the inflamed and bitter enemies of to-morrow.

My Lord and Gentlemen of the British Commission, we want you to return to England realizing how difficult and complex is the task of our President. Under our system of government, he alone can speak for the nation and commit us in our foreign relations, upon him alone is imposed the awful burden of responsibility and duty, and patriotism commands us as Americans loyally to support him, whatever may be our individual opinions or sentiments as to particular measures or grave omissions. We want you to return profoundly convinced that in standing by our policy of neutrality, we are not indifferent, or callous, or pusillanimous, or mercenary; and that our President is striving on our behalf to do what is right as God gives him to see the right, not only by the Americans now living but by those future generations for whom we are the trustees. Above all, we want you to return to England firmly believing that we unqualifiedly approve and extol the noble and heroic action of England in drawing her sword in defense of Belgium, and that our heartfelt sympathy and good wishes are with you and your heroic sailors and soldiers at the front.

Gentlemen, I ask you to rise and lift your glasses high and drain them in honor of the distinguished representatives of England. I have the pleasure of presenting to you the Right Honourable Lord Reading, the Lord Chief Justice of England.

INDEX